The Long Vacation

Alex (age 13) after the war
in Memmingen, Germany

The Long Vacation

A Memoir

Alex Panasenko

Iris Press
Oak Ridge, Tennessee

COVER PHOTOGRAPH:
A German woman carrying a few possessions runs from burning building in Siegburg, Germany. The fire started by Nazi saboteur.
—The U.S. National Archives and Records Administration

BOOK DESIGN:
Robert B. Cumming, Jr.

Library of Congress Cataloging-in-Publication Data

Names: Panasenko, Alex, 1933- author.
Title: The long vacation : a memoir / Alex Panasenko.
Description: Oak Ridge, Tennessee : Iris Press, [2020]
Identifiers: LCCN 2020008014 | ISBN 9781604542622 (paperback) | ISBN
    9781604548143 (ebook)
Subjects: LCSH: Panasenko, Alex, 1933- | World War,
    1939-1945—Youth—Ukraine. | World War, 1939-1945—Youth—Germany. |
    World War, 1939-1945—Conscript labor—Germany. | World War,
    1939-1945—Personal narratives, Ukrainian. |
    Ukrainians—Germany—Biography. | Kharkiv (Ukraine)—Biography.
Classification: LCC D810.Y74 P36 2020 | DDC 940.53/4775092 [B]—dc23
LC record available at https://lccn.loc.gov/2020008014

To those of my age group
who started this trip with me
but never arrived

Acknowledgments

Numerous persons are to be credited for the publication of this book. I am the least of them. I wrote it solely to get unpleasant memories out of my mind and on to paper, planning to banish them to a dusty cardboard box in the cellar.

But a few friends and ex-students expressed interest in the thing, so I let them read it. They all suggested that I get it published. I never made an effort to do so.

My friends persisted. Evelyn Frickel and Simon Max Hill typed and converted the original, cursive-covered sheets into neatly typed pages and a PDF. I thank them for that.

Most of the credit for motivating me to move on the project belongs to Christine Parkhurst, who submitted the manuscript to Iris Press. Thank you, Christine.

I thank my copyreader Cathy Kodra for her sharp eye, attention to detail, thorough review, and gentle editing suggestions. Also thanks to Mickey Ronningen for proofreading and editing suggestions.

Thanks to Sidney Hall, Jr. and Lesley Bruynesteyn for editing the Introduction and for helpful input.

I am greatly indebted to Beto and Bob Cumming, publishers at Iris Press, for their encouragement and help, careful editing, and for shepherding the project to completion. To Beto for the book design. Thank you both.

Finally, I wish to thank my wife Sally Fuller Panasenko, who spent many hours researching historical sources and background related to events I mention in the book. She also provided technical support and encouragement by prodding me through the process of rewriting and editing.

My sincere gratitude goes out to all the above-mentioned people as well as to those whose input I may have forgotten.

Introduction

This remembrance was never meant to be published. Some of the events described herein made a bit of an impression on me while I was still of an age when things are not readily rationalized. Coming from a culture where a man is expected to handle his problems without "professional" help, I tried. For decades, I enriched brewers and distillers and kept company with many ladies. When these traditional methods failed, I hit on the idea of writing it all down in hopes of thus transferring unpleasant memories to paper where, like government promises, they would soon be forgotten.

And so, in the early 1990s, I sat down and filled many pages with cursive handwriting. Even though I was doing this between correcting essay exams and planning lessons for my A.P. Biology classes at Berkeley High School, I completed the project in only a few weeks. And to a considerable degree, it worked.

Some years later, I received a call from a woman from the Oregon Jewish Museum in Portland who wanted to interview me about my experiences. I told her I was not Jewish and had been in a work camp, not a concentration camp. She informed me that I was nevertheless considered a "survivor," and so the interview took place. I found it difficult to sleep the night before. It was not so much that I was forced to recall various unpleasant occurrences, but that the act of doing so took me back in time and made me feel as helpless and frightened as I did then.

I also feel sensitive about the term "survivor." In no way can my situation be equated with that of people who made it through Buchenwald or Dachau. We had no barbed-wire fence, no machine-gun towers. We were penned in somewhat like domestic animals, but on Sundays we could leave to attend church. Perhaps our guards were more like herders or keepers. The beatings we received were fairly mild by the standards of the times, and while the food was skimpy and of horrid quality, I suspect that our own people who ran the kitchen had something to do with that.

The overriding consideration was our official subhuman status. I distinctly recall seeing us referred to in the German media as *Das wiederliche Untermenschentum*, which translates into "repulsive sub-humanity." Mostly we were called *Ostarbeiter*, meaning "Eastern workers," the "eastern" defining our subhuman condition and differentiating us from forced laborers who came from truly human countries like Holland or France.

Almost any German could do damn near anything to any one of us. Having anything to do with a German female bought us a one-way ticket to a concentration camp. Add to that Stalin's declaration that we had betrayed the Soviet Union by allowing the Germans to put us to work, and would probably be killed or imprisoned upon our return to the Soviet Union, and one can see why we were stressed, insecure, and fearful.

I was born in 1933 in Kharkov, Ukraine, in the midst of an artificial famine brought on by Stalin's policy of collectivization. Beginning in 1929, Ukrainian peasants were stripped of their land, livestock, and equipment and forced to work on government-run farms called *kolkhozes*. The peasants were understandably not happy about this. Many rose up, refused to harvest crops, slowed down production, and failed to maintain machinery. Large numbers attempted to relocate from the farms to other areas so that they could support themselves, but the NKVD restricted their movement, dooming them to their fate. Still others were expelled to Siberia and other barren lands east of the Urals as punishment.

The 1932 harvest was drastically diminished as a result. Ukraine's fertile *chernozem* (black earth) was experiencing a man-made famine of epic proportion. Nevertheless, Stalin exported large amounts of grain to finance his other projects. Not enough food remained to sustain the population. But even as the peasants began to starve, Stalin rejected any offers of outside aid.

Urban areas were also severely impacted as their rations were drastically cut. In addition to exporting large amounts of the harvest, Stalin sent in special commandos to raid private homes and confiscate food and livestock from starving families. In 1932-1933, when my mother was pregnant with me, the famine was at its peak, and people were dropping dead in our streets. Tens of thousands were starving to death each day. Conditions were so bad that some turned to cannibalism to survive. By the time I was born in September, millions had died of starvation. The lifespan of a male born in Kharkov in 1933 was only 7.5 years.

Back then, it was referred to as simply the Great Famine. Today it is called *Holodomor* (murder by starvation). In 1990, an international commission determined that a minimum of 4.5 million Ukrainians died of starvation during that time. Since 2006, it has been recognized by 16 countries, including the United States, as a genocide of the Ukrainian people perpetrated by the Soviet government.

My family somehow survived. For a time, we were fine. My father, a PhD in Mycology, taught at the Kharkov Agriculture Institute. My mother, a PhD in Slavic literature, also taught. I passed the time as children do, playing with other children, some of whose parents had been liquidated, and learning interesting skills and life lessons from our household help.

Meanwhile, the Great Purge lurked in the background. From 1936 to 1938, Stalin conducted massive, systematic purges across the Soviet Union to eliminate any possible enemies, particularly Communist Party members whom he deemed disloyal. Hundreds of thousands were executed. Millions more were exiled to Gulags in Siberia. Included in Stalin's sights were many of his top military officers, summarily executed. An estimated 30,000 officers were killed, including 90 percent of the generals and 80 percent of the colonels. Others were arrested or exiled.

We survived the Great Purge and life went on. In 1938, my brother was born, and I started kindergarten. Then in 1939, Germany invaded Poland, and World War II began. Things started to fall apart again.

In June 1941, Hitler launched Operation Barbarossa, the largest and most powerful military operation in history. More than 3 million personnel, 3,300 tanks, 7,000 artillery pieces, and hundreds of thousands of other types of vehicles and horses crossed the 2,900-kilometer border between Germany and the Soviet Union.

The *Einsatzgruppen* (SS execution squads) followed the army, massacring civilians as they went. Jews, Roma, the mentally and physically handicapped, and political opponents were their targets. Some of World War II's largest battles, casualties, and most horrific atrocities occurred at the Eastern Front during that time.

Stalin was completely unprepared for the invasion. Even as millions of German troops were amassing at the border, he remained convinced that Hitler would honor the German-Soviet non-aggression pact. Roosevelt, Churchill, and Stalin's spies warned him, but the Soviet dictator distrusted their motives and stubbornly believed the Germans wouldn't fight on two fronts. Due to Stalin's lack of preparation and destroyed officer corps, the Red Army was caught flat-footed and quickly overrun by Hitler and his allies.

The Wehrmacht rapidly advanced through Ukraine. Western cities, including Lviv, fell in late June, and in July and August others rapidly followed. Kiev fell on September 26. The tsunami of war headed right at us, with not much in place to hold it back.

Hitler's plan for the Soviet Union was to convert the European part of it, particularly Ukraine, the "breadbasket of Europe," into *Lebensraum* (living space) for German settlers. He despised the Slavic people, considering them subhuman and fit only for manual labor. He wrote in *Mein Kampf* that Germany's historical destiny was in the East. Indeed the Nazis claimed the German people possessed a genetic urge to colonize eastern territories, "*der Drang nach Osten.*" To fulfill his plan, he would carry out ethnic cleansing on an unprecedented scale. He planned to murder, starve to death, expel, sterilize, or enslave the majority of Russian and other Slavic populations and repopulate the land with millions of Germans under the *Generalplan Ost.*

As part of this, millions of Ukrainians, including my family, were forcibly deported from Ukraine to Germany for slave labor. Millions more were killed during World War II, many of them by the returning Red Army, who viewed them as traitors for not having fled before the German advance.

My story, seen through the eyes of a young boy and recorded many years later, is only a small part of the larger tale.

—Alex Panasenko
Portland, Oregon 2020

I

In my father's camp was a biochemist whom everyone disliked. He was reputedly brilliant, or at least very good at chess. They were mostly Russians in my father's camp, and all it takes to pass for brilliant among the Russians is to play a good game of chess and wash behind the ears.

The biochemist was a dwarf. He was an ugly, hunchbacked creature who read Alexandr Block and smoked cigarette butts, which the Germans would throw away. He smoked them in a long cigarette holder which gave him a certain style. Perhaps he *was* brilliant. They were all scientists, at my father's camp, whom the Wehrmacht had removed from the USSR and put to work in a special research camp in Austria. The Soviet government considered them to be collaborators and had condemned them to death, in absentia.

When the Red Army approached in 1945, the dwarf called his colleagues together in an-out-of-the-way shed. He had set up a distilling apparatus over an alcohol burner. He had saved up what cigarette butts he had picked up over the past several weeks. Since he was addicted to smoking, chess, and Alexandr Block, this must have been quite a sacrifice for him. He had soaked the cigarette butts in water and now was distilling the brown liquid.

"Our German masters are getting their asses kicked," said the dwarf. "They will run away and leave us to the mercy of our relatives over there." He nodded towards the east where Soviet artillery could faintly be heard. "I suggest we kill ourselves with nicotine. I am distilling it now. A small drop kills almost instantly."

My father and the other Russians listened attentively. Then they retreated with the Germans and after the war lost themselves in the maze of displaced persons' camps. The dwarf took his nicotine and died. Perhaps he simply had a bad case of nicotine addiction.

I was reminded of the story many years later in the '70s when I read the *The Anarchist Cookbook*. It said that the CIA used concentrated nicotine to assassinate people, as the effects were rather like a heart attack. I got a bottle but couldn't think of anyone I wanted to assassinate. The bottle is around someplace in case I ever think of someone. It's good to be prepared for those things. I also intend to read some Alexandr Block before I forget how to read Russian.

Compared to my father's camp, where inmates were never beaten and received rations comparable to those of the German civilians, my camp was a dump. It contained garbage people. True *Untermenschen,* as the few old and crippled guards never tired of pointing out to us. Most of the slave laborers were women, or "useless intellectuals," in other words, people with liberal arts degrees that were of no use to the war effort, or kids like myself, though I was by far the youngest. We worked in the fields and vineyards. We ate potato soup, and when a guard or an Austrian farmer caught us woolgathering, we got the living shit beaten out of us.

I resented being there. I also felt superior to my fellow subhumans. They were a pitiful lot. The women were wrinkled and ugly (or at least they appear that way in retrospect). The men were the sort of characterless, emasculated trash that survives great calamities. These people had survived Stalin's purges by informing on their friends, and they attempted to survive this iniquity by informing on one another. But the Germans didn't give a fuck about dialectic materialism. The Germans were only interested in getting the maximum work out of us.

Krupp and I.G. Farben Industrie ran labor camps that were paragons of their kind. The inmates were beaten with steel whips, castrated, and in other ways made to realize their low evolutionary status. To have survived one of those camps would place one in the category of survivors of Buchenwald or Matthausen. Those places were the Cadillacs, the Lincoln Continentals. My place was a Ford Pinto.

It is heartbreaking to realize from the beginning that one is being groomed for a life of mediocrity. Except at the very beginning, I was destined to be one of the elite and have managed to escape that fate by the sheerest circumstance.

I was born in 1933 in Kharkov in eastern Ukraine. At that time people were dropping dead in the streets as a result of Stalin's artificially instituted famine (*Holodomor*), caused by his collectivization of the farms. Now it is 1993, and people are still dropping dead in the streets in various parts of the world. So, I am still adjusted to my environment. I still belong.

Since only a boor does not mention his parents, I will mention mine and quickly move on. My father was a Cossack, the first of his family to set aside his saber (not, however, until he got tired of using it during the Russian Revolution) and get a college degree. Indeed, the poor man got a PhD., proving as it turned out that a little knowledge is a dangerous thing. My father's PhD. was in Mycology (molds, fungi, and mushrooms); my mother's was in Slavic literature. It is because of his PhD. that the Germans considered him useful and we wound up in our respective camps.

Before the war, life was glorious. My parents were always gone to fulfill tasks set them by the Communist Party in far corners of the USSR. I was left with an old alcoholic cook and a near illiterate eighteen-year-old "domestic worker." This was not bad for living in a classless society.

The cook taught me to steal food at the open-air farmers' market, and this enabled her to take the money reserved for shopping and buy vodka. The eighteen-year-old tried to interest me in her pussy. It was big, hairy, and wet and scared the crap out of me. In self-defense, I must add that I was six years old at the time. Had she but waited two years, I might have caught the clap at the age of eight.

Whenever the pleasures of stealing and voyeur sex failed, there were always homeless kids to play with. Their parents had been liquidated for various political mistakes, and the kids lived in cellars and hallways until the State rounded them up like wild animals.

It was with one of them, a girl named Sonja, that I fell in love for the first time in my life. But poor Sonja had lice. She asked me if I wanted to see "it" and when I nodded, took me down for a closer look. There, right in front of my spellbound nose, was a tiny gray insect burrowing into delectably pink labia. The romance faltered and died.

There were always NKVD troopers walking around in pairs wearing raspberry collar tabs and hatbands on their uniforms. We would run up to them and ask them to show us their pistols and tell us about how many people they had liquidated. We never got to see a gun and were generally treated with kind vulgarity ("Get the fuck away from me, kids, or I will go home with you and liquidate your motherfucking family"). Life was an intriguing adventure full of possibilities.

There was, of course, kindergarten. It was a special kindergarten for children of Party members and intellectual workers. I was driven there in a car now and then. My street friends, who had only seen a car from the outside, envied me this experience.

Once past its magical doors, the kindergarten provided us with glimpses into mathematics, history of the Party, lessons in ballet, rifle marksmanship, and lectures on how to turn our parents in to the NKVD.

One day we were visited by an actual NKVD officer. He smiled a lot, told us that Comrade Stalin loved every one of us, and said that some of our parents might be confused and might say bad things about Comrade Stalin. If that happened, he said, we should tell our teacher about it, and things would be explained to the parents.

For a special treat, the teacher read us passages from *The Adventures of Huckleberry Finn* and explained that this was life in present-day America where they "sold their black people." The idea that there were black people intrigued me at the time. It also led to the first of my many confrontations with authority. I stood up and accused the teacher of lying.

"There are no black people," I said, and turning to the class, I asked if any of them had ever seen a black person. The answer was a resounding "no," which destroyed much of the poor woman's credibility. She brought in a book with pictures the next day, but seeds of distrust had already been planted.

The idea of selling people did not seem all that different from turning in parents to have them liquidated.

Due to the favored status of our kindergarten, we got to go to summer camp. It lasted for two weeks and included lessons in communist ideology and lots of nature walks. Left to ourselves, we collected bugs, stole apples from a nearby orchard, and played a game of "NKVD and spies." This consisted of choosing a victim by lot, hitting him, and screaming, "Confess you bastard!" Once the victim could not take it anymore, he would scream, "I confess!" whereupon he was shot in the back of the head with a cap pistol, and the next spy would be chosen.

The war arrived just a little before grammar school. Of the two, the school had a more immediate and frightening impact. We were assigned to two-person desks arranged in the sequence of boy-girl, girl-boy, and boy-girl. There were inkwells inset into the desktops. The girl next to me was a timid, mousy brunette. The girl in front was a stuck-up little blonde with a thick pigtail.

I have always been influenced, led, and misled by women ever since the eighteen-year-old imprinted me with her bush. So when my little deskmate whispered a suggestion in my ear, I took the blonde's pigtail and dunked it in the inkwell.

Retaliation was swift. The blonde shrieked like a pig in a slaughterhouse. The teacher, a NOW virago born before her time, sent me home with a devastating letter attached to my jacket.

That night my father beat me to a bloody pulp, and we had our first air raid.

My mother woke me up in the middle of the night. There was a loud banging, and I tried to go back to sleep. Probably, that would have been the sanest and safest thing to do. For the first few weeks, the air raids were simply recognizance flights. The only danger was from falling shell fragments from the horrific anti-aircraft barrages the Soviets put up. But, of course, mothers always know best, so off we went, walking the length of a city block to our designated shelter, while the falling steel fragments struck sparks off the cobblestones all around us. We sat in a cavernous cellar, its ceiling supported by Romanesque brick columns while the Russian babushkas sat around and muttered, "Terrible, terrible."

It was around this time that I learned to hate air raid shelters. In the USSR, and later in Germany, I found them to be simply deathtraps. If the brick building above them collapsed from a bomb, no one usually bothered to dig out the survivors. Walking about German streets in April of 1945, one could smell the contents of numerous air raid shelters moldering away.

But that first night it was all new and strangely disagreeable. I tried to go back to sleep but couldn't. The next day, cranky from lack of sleep, I rendered a lengthy apology to the ink-stained blonde and was seated far away from her in a remote corner. The feminist hag teacher gave a long speech about the invincibility of the mighty Red Army and the wisdom of Comrade Stalin. Then she sent us home.

I did not enter a classroom again for seven years.

The air raids intensified, and we stopped going to the shelter. People started talking about the crowded refugee trains that were passing through the area. Military transport going west had priority, and the trains would stand about for hours and days with the people on them afraid to get off in case the train started again. They would beg passersby to give them water.

About this time, all the men who had not been called up for military service were ordered out of town to dig anti-tank ditches. My father left, so I no longer had to be constantly frightened. There was still the war and the air raids, but I no longer had to worry about beatings for minor transgressions.

One night I was sitting at the living room table with my mother while the anti-aircraft fired away outside. There was an unearthly howl followed by a tremendous concussion. The house shook, and dust rose.

"That was a bomb," said Mother. "Get under the table."

She got my three-year-old brother, and we huddled under the table while things went bang outside.

That was the first and the closest German bombing raid I lived through. In the morning, several houses in the neighborhood were gone, replaced by piles of rubble and huge craters. Various belongings were scattered about. During all my years and wars, I never got over how pitiful, how horribly pathetic, a personal belonging appears when it is tossed aside by an act of war. Corpses lost their humanity and became mere things to be ignored, but a child's toy or a woman's cooking pot that had been something prized and used only hours ago filled me with sadness.

Following the bombing raid, the district Party committees made everyone dig slit trenches in the back yards. Ours was a beauty. It was planned by some World War I veterans with knowledge of such things. It was L-shaped and covered with streetcar rails, boards, and much dirt. There was a long bench that could accommodate about a dozen people. I liked to sit in it even when there wasn't a raid.

Soon the bombing became a nightly event. It was beautiful. I would watch the multicolored tracers streaking up into the projector beam-checkered sky and dream of being a pilot. Invulnerable, I would possess the fickle power to push a button and obliterate everyone beneath me. It is true that during several months of German bombing, I did not see a single German plane shot down, while the city beneath them died in spite of hundreds of anti-aircraft guns.

How different it would be years later when I saw American Flying Fortresses flame in the German sky, shedding their wings and metamorphosing into junk.

But that time was still light years away. I spent my days happily adding to my fragment collection and classifying shell fragments (long and thin), and bomb fragments (chunkier and thicker). I even had that most desirable of all things, a nosecone from a shell. It was black and had a silver rim along the bottom on which were mysterious numbers, like runes of some dark power.

About that time, I turned eight and became somewhat of a player. I had two girlfriends. The first, Sarah, was a red-haired Jewish girl with freckles.

One day she ran up to me and screamed, "You are an abnormal psycho!"

I was struck by her sophisticated vocabulary. "Fuck you!" I replied.

"That is a horrible word and shows disrespect to your mother," she said.

"I won't use it if you show me your pussy," I said.

"I can't," she said, "I am wearing panties, but if someday my mother doesn't make me wear them, I will." That settled it. We had a relationship.

The other girl was called Marussia. She was small and blonde. We had a secret meeting in the cellar of her house which contained a large pickle barrel lying on its side. We crawled into the pickle barrel, and I went down on Marussia and started licking. I had never heard about oral sex from anyone. I just did it. She seemed to be quite enthusiastic about the project and, male ego and the inaccuracy of old memories aside, I am certain that she was bucking and thrusting her skinny self against me.

Her grandfather, a courtly old gentleman, caught us and was shocked speechless. Like most primitive people, the Russians of that era were horrified by oral sex, which they viewed as perversion. I was dragged by my ear to my home where the old gent told my mother that I had been doing "unspeakable things" and departed. When pressed for an explanation, I admitted to kissing the girl and was told to stand in the corner for five minutes.

Poor Sarah, poor Marussia. The Germans killed Sarah, and Marussia died in a famine that winter.

In our central yard was a large sandbox used by the younger kids for play and by the neighborhood cats for sanitary purposes. One day a group of us were playing war by placing sand in newspaper squares, twisting the paper around the sand, and throwing the results at each other. The paper bundles flew through the air, leaving a fine trail of sand that resembled a tracer trail produced by anti-aircraft projectiles. We were so involved in this occupation that we failed to hear the approach of a plane.

Suddenly a horrible banging arose as nearby batteries opened up. We looked up and there, low enough to be seen, was a single-engine plane. Painted pale blue and gray, it had tiny black crosses on its wings. It made several graceful turns with the explosions of anti-aircraft shells following and then flew away. Its engine sounded totally alien, very different from the dry, crackling sound of Soviet planes. At that precise point, I realized that we were losing the war.

The next week the invincible Red Army started to withdraw through our town. Long columns of cavalry and horse-drawn wagons clattered down a cobbled street that led to the river and bridge. The bridge was mined, and armed sentries stood at either end. I walked up to one of them.

"Is that a real grenade on your belt?" I asked.

"It motherfucking sure is, kid," the sentry said.

"How do you make it go off?" I asked.

The sentry leaned his rifle against the bridge, pulled out the grenade, and started giving me a lecture on how to use the Soviet hand grenade. The sentry's officer showed up.

"What the fuck do you think you are doing, Ivanov?" he asked.

"Showing the kid how to kill fucking Germans, Comrade Lieutenant."

"You want to kill Germans, kid?" the lieutenant asked.

Inhibited by all this attention, I nodded shyly.

"Good kid," said the lieutenant, and, handing me a cigarette, he walked away.

"Do you smoke, kid?" the sentry asked.

I said no, I did not.

"Does your father smoke?"

I said no, he did not. "You better give me that cigarette, then," said the sentry. "Fucking officers don't know what's good for kids, anyway." He fumbled in a pocket and looked confused. "You don't carry matches with you, do you?"

I said I did not. He put my cigarette in his shirt pocket, carefully rebuttoning the flap.

"Say, kid, you don't have an older sister, do you?"

Regretfully, I told him all I had was a younger brother. Then I added that we had had a serving girl and a cook, but that they had gone home when the war started.

"Your father must be somebody important," said the sentry. "Is he a Party member?"

I shamefully admitted I had no idea but that my father taught at a university.

"So you must be educated, too. Can you write your name?" he asked.

I picked up a stick and wrote my name in the wet sand by the river.

"Alexandr," the soldier said. "I have a brother named Alexandr. That is an important coincidence."

That it certainly was. About one-quarter of all the Russians that I knew were named Alexandr, another quarter were named Konstantin, another third were Ivans, and those left shared all the other names.

The sentry was about to prove he could write his name as well as any eight-year-old, but his lieutenant came up again and told him to get back to guarding the bridge.

Soon my father returned from digging the anti-tank ditches. He looked gray and shrunken. We had another huge air raid. The morning after, there was a woman's leg in our backyard. I saw it first. It was very white and very shapely. It had been torn off at the hip. It wore a black silk stocking and even had a high-heeled shoe. I felt intensely sexually excited by it and also guilty for feeling excited. My father buried it. The next morning, there it was again looking much the worse for wear and not exciting at all. The morning after, the story repeated itself. My father put it in a sack and took it somewhere.

About this time, the government began destroying its files. There was a constant smell of burning, and tiny pieces of ash floated down on everything and everyone. We received our evacuation tickets to go east, beyond the Ural Mountains. By this time, neither trains nor road transport could move by daylight due to German dive-bombers. We decided to stay. My parents emulated the Party by burning lots of their papers.

Unexpectedly, the air raids came to an end. German planes were overhead most of the time, but not a single bomb fell. The Party began to organize a workers' militia, and posters appeared on all walls urging people to form partisan units in the German rear. The posters pictured a middle-aged, mustachioed, stern-visaged man in a railroad or streetcar conductor's cap, with a romantic looking bandolier across his chest, flinging a hand grenade at a line of German trucks whose canvas-shrouded sides were obligingly decorated with a swastika.

"Form partisan detachments. Go to your local Party office for weapons and instructions," read the posters.

My friends and I went to watch the training of the local militia. About two hundred malnourished-looking men sat in a huddled gray herd along one side of a soccer field. A bored, uniformed army soldier stood by the goalposts, holding a long pole to one end of which a soccer ball had been attached. An equally bored army officer conducted the training. This entire herd of men had only one rifle between them.

Russian rifles of that era (Mosin-Nagant Model 91/30) were long, rather unwieldy, with a spike bayonet semi-permanently attached to the muzzle. The militiamen would take the rifle in turn and would jog in a tired and dispirited way around the periphery of the field. When they returned to the goalposts, the army soldier would thrust at them with the ball on the end of the stick. They had to parry the thrust with the rifle and then stick the bayonet into a sack, filled with something, that had been tied to one of the goalposts. The bored officer offered instructions and encouragement after first consulting a long roster for the name of the trainee.

"What's the fucking matter with you, Yefremov? Why did you let that soldier punch your fucking face with that fucking ball? You had the rifle. Parry, you prick!"

"You shake your ass like a fucking whore when you are running, Dozhenko! You going to fight the Germans or fuck them?"

This provoked laughter from the assembled trainees.

"I beg your pardon, Comrade Commander, but I am not Dozhenko," offered the ass-shaker.

"Ah, who gives a fuck? Sit down. Who's next?" said the officer.

Somehow one did not feel well-protected by this bunch.

Trenches and bunkers were now constructed along the sides of the major streets. The streets themselves had rows of rusty tank obstacles lined up across them, leaving only narrow passages that allowed one car to pass at a time. The obstacles were made of railroad rails welded together in a sort of X.

Red Army units were still retreating through town, with the civilian population milling about in an agitated mood. The people didn't know what to expect and tried to question the soldiers.

"Are you retreating, comrade?"

"Hell no, Mother, we are just changing our positions. We are kicking the shit out of the Fritzes. They are running back to Berlin."

It was like a futuristic off-Broadway play, this double-think, double-speak communication, evolved after twenty years of Party rule and political correctness. No one could speak the objective truth upon pain of drastic punishment, yet in a painfully convoluted way, the truth was spoken. We were getting wiped out. The Germans were winning. Everything I had been told by the adults in kindergarten had been a lie. The glorious Red Army was a pack of losers and even Comrade Stalin in all his power and glory, and even the NKVD with all its sinister knowledge, could do nothing.

It was a frightening and wondrously liberating sensation. I had been right in suspecting them all along. I was right, and they were wrong. At the age of eight, I had attained the mania of greatness.

I shared my views on this cataclysmic revelation with Sarah when I met her carrying a chicken. The chicken's legs were tied with a stout bit of twine and Sarah was using this for a handle, carrying the hen upside down. I accompanied her around the back of some houses to a small shack.

A tiny, bent, walleyed man opened the door. Behind him was a long tin basin filled with blood. Chickens and ducks, with their necks severed, hung by their feet above the basin, dripping their last drops. The little man carried a shiny straight razor. Sarah handed him the hen, and we went outside.

"They lied," I said, "All the teachers lied, and my parents lied. None of it is true, and the Germans are winning. Comrade Stalin is stupid, and the Red Army is running away."

This was an outrageously bold speech for the time. People were getting turned in and arrested, never to be seen again, for much less. So I was surprised and offended when Sarah failed to respond in any of the several ways I had expected. Instead she looked troubled and sad.

"My parents say the Germans will kill us," she said.

"It's all lies," I said. "The government lies, like about the war."

"It's not the government. The government isn't saying anything. We know from other Jews. They are killing all of us."

I did not believe one word of this. It seemed too outrageous. But I did note that she was right about one thing. I could not recall hearing a single word from official sources about the Germans killing Jews.

The little man now came out of the shack and handed Sarah her chicken. She gave him two grimy ruble bills, and we walked back to her home.

Neither of us said anything. A sudden chasm had appeared between us. She was Jewish. I was Ukrainian. That was all there was to it. Like day and night in the biblical Genesis, we were separated by a line, terrible in its unalterable simplicity.

The next and last time I saw her, she was in a drab, pathetic line guarded by smiling Germans.

When I got home, there was an army car outside the door. In the kitchen sat three officers. They all had mustaches and wore shiny belts with pistol holsters. One had a star with a hammer and sickle embroidered on his sleeve, denoting that he was a political commissar.

It turned out that they were distant relatives of my mother's. They said whatever it is that adults say to children to me. I said whatever it is that children say to adults to them. They were drinking vodka, and I was offered a tiny sip in the bottom of a glass. I looked at my mother for permission, and after she nodded, I tossed it off and made a face. They told me I had the makings of a Cossack. They left soon after that, leaving us a large case of tinned sardines.

That night my older half-brother showed up. He was my father's son but hated him and liked my mother. He wore the drab field uniform of a lieutenant.

"I can't stay long," he said, kissed my mother, and left. After the war, we heard that he had been killed in the battle of Berlin.

The next day the retreating Soviets started to burn the city, and my father went into hiding so he would not be mobilized on the spot by the retreating troops.

I stood in our backyard and watched the huge Kharkov Tractor Plant across the river going up in flames. The fire flowed like a golden liquid, writhed like a snake. Particles of soot floated in the air. A large barrage balloon with nets hanging from it that had been moored above the factory came loose and slowly drifted away.

A big kid named Zhora came by carrying what appeared to be an empty keg with something white on the bottom.

"They are robbing the stores," said Zhora.

"Who is robbing the stores?" I asked, horribly confused.

"Everybody, all the people," said Zhora.

"What about the militia?" I asked, "Why don't the soldiers stop them?"

"There are no soldiers," said Zhora. "Everything is allowed now."

"What have you got there?" I asked.

"Salt," said Zhora. "There are at least five kilograms of salt left in here, maybe ten. I can make pickles now if I can get some cucumbers."

He went away. None of my friends liked him because he was fucking a girl our age. She said that it hurt, but he gave her some money. He also offered money to one of my friends to stick his dick either into the kid's mouth or ass. Other kids of his age didn't want to have anything to do with him. We thought him either outright crazy or very odd and were afraid of him.

My father reappeared. He looked pale and frightened and carried a large sack on his back. The sack contained a combination of cattle feed that my father's agricultural college was experimenting with. We put it in a large closet in the back of the kitchen.

It was to save our lives.

At the beginning of the war, everyone had been required to turn in their radios. (Radios in the USSR had to be registered.) I did not miss ours very much because I was never allowed to listen to anything but classical music. The private radios had been replaced with public address systems whose huge rectangular speakers were bolted to telephone poles in every neighborhood, square, and public place.

These speakers would emit death rattle-like sounds and bellow out announcements and decrees, sometimes preceded or followed by martial music.

Now they all fell silent. The only sounds heard in the city were the explosions of demolition and the distant thunder of artillery. They were far more eloquent than any Party speaker, anyway.

News somehow got around, seemingly just as rapidly as when the loudspeakers were functioning. All of the families that lived in our block of flats knew to gather in our slit trench at about the same time.

On one such occasion, we gathered and then sat and waited. There was a sense of anticipation. Something new was going to happen. Something none of those present had ever experienced before.

The thing that happened was an intense blast of air that picked me up off the bench where I had been sitting and threw me bodily against the walls of the trench. I never cease to be amazed at how something as soft and invisible as air could suddenly grow fists and talons with which to pry you off the floor of a cellar or the bottom of a foxhole, lift you a considerable distance, and smash you against some hard surface.

I picked myself up and sat down again. A woman sitting near the end of the trench stuck her head out and told us that the bridge across the river had been blown. She then produced a pair of binoculars and, peering through them, told us there was a company of infantry taking up positions across the river.

"Put away those binoculars, you stupid bitch!" yelled some of the women. "They will think you are German and shell us." An argument now developed as to whether our trench looked too military and thus subject to attack.

Most of us moved into the cellar. Some stayed in the trench. I fell asleep and woke up to the sound of small-arms fire. Some of the adults were identifying the sounds of the different weapons.

I listened with interest. While it was very difficult to tell the rifles apart, it was quite easy to identify the machine guns. The German one had a very rapid snarling sound with the detonations of the individual shots merging into one. Our Maxim, by contrast, had a slow, measured stutter with the individual shots being readily discernible.

After a while, the adults' conversation veered to speculating about what life would be like under the Germans. I lost interest and went back to the corner occupied by my family.

They were all asleep, huddled under two blankets. My father was snoring and my kid brother made whimpering noises. The cellar smelled of rot, pickles, and sweat. In another corner, a woman was crying, and a man cursed monotonously. I went outside.

It was a sunny day. Pale autumn sunlight illuminated the yard. I sat on the step leading to the cellar door, a brick wall on my right and another staircase leading to the second floor on my left. I felt quite protected. I could spy on the war with impunity.

The war was all around. I was immersed in it. I breathed it in and sweated it out. There was a whirring in the air, a whistling and sighing, as invisible projectiles crossed each other's paths above our backyard. I was transfixed, spellbound. I never wanted it to end. I wanted to sit in my protected corner forever.

Suddenly, several Germans ran into the yard. They wore gray-green uniforms with dark green collars and steel helmets. They set up a short length of pipe attached to a heavy square base and started twirling small adjustment wheels. The pipe moved this way and that in response.

One of the Germans turned his head and saw me. He said something, and one of the other Germans came walking towards me while speaking in German and moving his hands the way one would shoo a chicken.

I was going to stand my ground. After all, I was a Cossack, this was my country, and he was a Fascist invader. Before all this resolve could be put to the test, however, one of the other Germans yelled something, and my German went back to rejoin his friends.

Another German now opened a square box and lifted out a perfectly shaped little yellow bomb. He put it into the front end of the pipe. I heard a *chunk*, and some pale, translucent smoke drifted out. The Germans repeated this four or five times, and then they took their weapons and ran out of the yard.

I walked over to see whether they had left anything. In particular, I was hoping they might have forgotten one of the bomblets, but nothing was there.

I went back into the cellar. Nothing much had changed there. My parents were still asleep, as was my brother who was now also sucking his thumb.

I went up to the cursing man with the crying wife.

"There were Germans out there, and I stood up to them. Then they ran away," I said.

The man gave me a disgusted look. "Get the fuck away from me. I have my own fucking problems," he said. Upon hearing the word "Germans," his wife started to cry louder. I went outside again.

The air still muttered, sobbed, whistled, and made ripping sounds. I felt more self-assured now that I had seen the Germans and they had not done anything to me. I decided to walk the few blocks to downtown and see what was happening.

The streets were completely empty. All the carefully constructed bunkers and trenches were also empty. The tank traps stood about, looking like discarded junk. At one point I heard engine noises, so I ducked into a doorway. Several trucks drove by with Germans in them. After they passed, I resumed my walk.

In a small park where I used to be taken by our "domestic worker" in happier days, I saw a German machine gun and several Germans. I looked at them, and they stared back at me. No one said anything.

The Red Square was a few streets further, flanked by all the important office buildings in town. There were three armored vehicles in the square. There was a light tank, turned completely upside down, an armored car that appeared to be undamaged, and a self-propelled gun on fire.

Three tankers were stuck in the hatch at the back of the self-propelled gun. Their faces and lips melted, and smoking black drops fell to the ground. I had never realized people could burn and melt. The realization that people were just things was shattering.

Just before the war, there had been a popular song, one of the stupid militaristic ditties probably written by some Party hack, about "three tankers—three happy comrades." This song kept running through my mind as I watched them melt and drip. Their teeth shone through the black remnants, a shocking canary yellow.

Years later in 1974, as I bar-hopped in San Francisco, I walked into a bookstore on Powell Street to look at some books and sober up a bit before heading for the Tenderloin area. There was a book on a bargain table, entitled *Russian Tanks 1900-1970* by John Milsom. Since it was only $3.95, I bought it. And there on page 129 was a picture of my tank. Not one like it, but the very same one. Standing in front of a ruined building, its back door open and corpses hanging out. The fire is out, and a German soldier with a rifle is walking past, looking at it. The text says it is a SU 45 self-propelled anti-tank gun and it was used against Finland. Well, that ain't Finland, John Milsom, and that ain't no Finnish soldier in the picture.

As a young boy, I had stood there for what seemed like a long time watching this scene. Then a German carrying a black weapon of a kind I had never seen before, but which I later learned was an MP-40 machine pistol, walked out from behind the undamaged armored car and started shouting incomprehensible words at me. He was very angry. I suppose he was concerned because the ammunition inside the tank could have exploded. I ran away.

The walk home was a blur. I kept thinking about the melting tankers. There were more Germans about now. The civilians had not yet come out. Several houses were burning, and there was still a great deal of shooting. Children lead charmed lives; so do idiots. I suppose I qualified in both categories.

When I got back to the cellar, everyone was awake and mad at me. My father slapped me a few times, and my mother started whining about how I was shortening her life and making her suffer. I felt reassured by all of this. Compared to melting tankers, I was way ahead.

Towards evening the firing died down. There was no more artillery. The first Battle of Kharkov was over. Having lost the city, the Red Army made a long, rapid withdrawal. Everyone was relieved. There was a sense of expectation. Strange, new things were going to happen. And they did.

2

That winter was the absolute low point of my life. There were others to follow: being in a labor camp and being dumped by wives and lovers without whom one tasted a terrible desolation, but those were things that happen to a very large number of normal people. What occurred in the winter of 1941-1942 in a couple of cities like Leningrad and Kharkov was reserved for the elect. Of course, I was too young, too insignificant, to have been one of the elect. I, in any event, lack the sort of arrogance, the sort of gall that it would take to claim the place of Job on the dunghill. But I must have stood somewhere near the elect when their fate was cast, and some of it settled on me.

The day after the Germans took the city, I awoke to find the streets outside shrouded in an autumnal fog. Echoing through the fog, I heard an ominous sound that was to be a part of my life for the next four years—the clacking of hob-nailed Wehrmacht boots on cobblestone streets.

I scrambled outside to observe the source of the sound. They appeared like creatures of the fog, emerging from the mist. They usually patrolled in pairs, outfitted with steel helmets, unfamiliar weapons, gray uniforms, and black cartridge belts. On the backs of the belts were small bags and flat bayonets. They wore cylindrical, fluted steel containers, which, I was to learn later, contained gas masks. Their faces were mostly distant and grim. They were immediately different, unmistakably alien. Compared to our soldiers, they were neater, cleaner, better equipped, better disciplined, and far less human.

Years later, I discovered myself acting in a distant and alien manner to other people in another war. So maybe the Germans were as human as we were, or perhaps they were merely as efficient at teaching as they seem to be at everything else. Certainly, they had more effect on my development than did any other group. And perhaps they still do.

These advancing German troops replaced the retreating Soviet troops. Long lines of German horse carts replaced long lines of Russian horse carts, all moving east.

Since water and electric facilities had been blown up by the retreating Russians, lines formed for the few wells that were still functional. The civilian population needed the water for drinking; the Germans needed it for their horses. This led to conflicts of interest. My father, while standing in line, observed a Russian, who also been waiting for several hours, finally get his bucket of water. A German walked up to him and tried to take it from him. The Russian refused. The German unceremoniously shot the Russian and calmly watered his horses. Germans were not only efficient; they also loved animals.

Two days after the Germans entered the city, my father took me for a walk. It essentially duplicated the walk I had taken by myself during the battle except that now the sun shone and the streets were crowded with lots of people, Germans and civilians alike.

My self-propelled gun was still there. The corpses had been removed, but the smell of burned flesh and diesel oil was still quite noticeable. I wanted to look inside to see if any of the ammunition had exploded, but my father wrinkled his nose in disgust and pulled me away.

We walked along the main street, past burned-out buildings and vehicles. The Soviet-installed public address system was operating as if nothing had changed.

"...and the noble German nation, without sparing the blood of its best sons, liberated us from the Jewish-Commissar menace..."

The woman's voice was exactly like that of her predecessors who had used the same phrases: "...the Soviet Union, without sparing the blood of its best sons...," etc. Possibly it was the same woman. She certainly spoke part of the truth. Neither nation gave the slightest thought to sparing the blood of anybody, including sons, daughters, fathers, mothers, infants, or barnyard animals.

We walked past the German headquarters. Two sentries stood in immobile perfection, saluting incoming officers with robotic enthusiasm. Two giant flags hung from windows above the main entry. One was the German swastika, the other the yellow and blue Ukrainian flag. I had never known that we had a flag, and seeing it did not impress me. It looked like a cheap bit of theatrical decoration. In any event, it disappeared soon after that and was not seen again.

Proclamations hung on walls telling people to turn in their firearms and explaining the theory of collective responsibility. As to firearms, no one was allowed to possess any under the Soviet system anyway, so that provision must have been easy to follow. As for collective responsibility, that was not difficult either. All one had to do was abide by the law.

At regular intervals, a German patrol would come by and collect one man from every tenth house on the street. The men were kept at a central location for a specified length of time. If during that time someone killed a German, ten of these law-abiding citizens would be taken out and hanged.

Since all public recreation facilities had been destroyed, those hangings were to provide us with entertainment, object moral lessons, and in many instances, a source of food.

That food would become the major problem soon became evident. The retreating Soviets had destroyed all food stores and burned all fields. Some tracts planted with sugar beets remained, but the Germans needed those to feed their horses, and when a horde of starving city dwellers went to dig them up, they were machine-gunned. A few of the better-looking women got jobs peeling potatoes for the German Army kitchens. They were allowed to keep the peels but had to screw the Germans who worked in the kitchens. (Why couldn't we have a set-up like that when I was pulling K.P. in the U.S. Army a mere eleven years later?)

As for the majority of us, we sat like laboratory rabbits in a cage after a lazy lab attendant forgets to put in a fresh supply of food pellets, and awaited the inevitable. First the dogs and cats disappeared, then the sparrows.

One day Zhora came by with a slingshot. He was hunting sparrows and seemed depressed. He said that his mother, who was as crazy as he was, had told him that she would "make soup out of him." He said she had a large knife.

A few days later I returned home from playing in the yard. My father was standing in the kitchen staring at me with a peculiar look on his face. After asking where I had been, he informed me that I had just killed our entire family. It seems when he was carrying the daily bucket of water from the well, he was followed by three Germans. They entered our apartment on his heels and methodically robbed us of all our emergency food: the sardines left by the Red Army officers, some sugar my mother had squirreled away, and our stash of tea. Because my kid brother had been home, the Germans left him a cup of sugar cubes. They had not believed my father when he told them he had another child.

My father proceeded to beat me about the face and head, repeating over and over, "We are all going to starve. It is all your fault. We are all going to starve!"

My mother later told me it was not really all my fault, but I was never quite certain. What appeared to be a dead certainty was more distressing: by then it had become common knowledge that the Germans considered us Slavs to be subhuman, (the generic term for us was *Untermenschen*) and themselves to be the bearers of culture, or *Kulturtrager*. My father's actions towards me indicated to me that the Germans were very likely correct in their assessment of us. Later in the camp, watching my elders and betters steal, beg, lie, inform, and die, I became convinced of it.

The Germans were brutal, inhuman, efficient, and loyal to a demented leader. Yet, on the whole, they were more honest and honorable in their personal dealings. They were not snide, lying, backstabbing weaklings. They told you what they were going to do and then they did it. And what they were going to do was wipe us out because they needed our land to support more Germans. The ecologists call it *habitat*; the Germans called it *Lebensraum*.

The winter of '41 set in early and hard. In front of Moscow, the German Army froze and died along with the concept of blitzkrieg.

In Leningrad, the civilians, surrounded by the German Army, starved by the millions and fed on their dead. In Kharkov, we starved by the thousands and ate the hostages the Germans obligingly hanged.

Bleak, cold, and dark dreariness was interrupted at times by events of crystalline surrealism that condensed and clarified our status in the new order. Perhaps they were that for me only, and those about me perceived them as simply manifestations of an indifferent beastliness.

One such surreal event was the behavior of our women. Before the echo of the last shot had faded, before the corpses had been buried or pushed out of the way, our women rushed forward to engulf the disdainful German troops in a sea of cunts, tongues, tits, and assholes. Their eyes shiny, their buttocks quivering, our women stalked the clean, disciplined boys of the Wehrmacht and submerged them in mucous lubricated flesh.

I later observed the same phenomenon to an even greater extent when the Americans entered the town I was in in Bavaria. It happened in Korea. And it was amply reported from Viet Nam.

Perhaps in our prehistory when one tribe defeated another and slaughtered all of its men, the females rushed forward to declare their sexual subservience and availability to the victors and thus survived, enjoyed, and in their turn, conquered. The male of any race is defined by his Y chromosome, which, although it carries few genes, carries the genes that determine maleness. Thus when the males died and the women survived, the male identity of the group was forever lost. The conquered women now replicated the victors' male identities. Men are expendable. Women are immortal.

On our block lived a policeman. He was a small, quiet man. I would see him going to work wearing his olive-drab uniform. I would smile at him, and he would smile at me. Once on duty, he would don a pistol belt and a white sun helmet with a multi-hued crest of the Soviet Union on its front. He would ascend a wooden pedestal and start directing traffic. I saw him several times at that occupation. Each time I would walk to the foot of the pedestal and look up at him. His eyes straight ahead, he grimly manifested Soviet law. I spent considerable time trying to determine whether it was the same man.

The policeman had a young wife and a barely teenage daughter. He didn't just love them; he was enslaved by them. When the Soviets retreated, instead of retreating with them as ordered, he deserted to be with his women. Because he was a policeman, he was afraid that his neighbors would denounce him to the Germans, as they in fact did, and so was hiding out in the city.

His apartment became an oasis of merriment on our dark and depressing block. A gramophone was constantly going, candles were lit, Germans were constantly going in and out, and the wife and daughter could be glimpsed dressed, half-dressed, or bare-ass naked through the windows.

One night we were all awakened by some truly horrid screams. The policeman had caught his women between Germans and took an ax to them. He didn't just kill them; he went on a regular spree, a chopping fest, until they were dead.

A German patrol arrived and looked the situation over. They took the ax out of the sobbing man's hands and shot him like a dog. It was probably an act of mercy.

All the Jews were rounded up and taken away. I was playing in the yard with some other kids when several uniformed Germans appeared. Without undue ceremony, they undid our flies and pulled out our little, chilled dicks. (In Russia only Jews are circumcised.) Unaware of the significance of the ceremony, I was acutely embarrassed, buttoning up my fly as one hapless boy was taken away.

Zhora's mother was turned in by her neighbors. There was a repulsive smell of boiling meat coming from her apartment. The neighbors broke in and discovered her boiling bits of Zhora. She was making soup "without any potatoes, or onions, or even salt," the boy who reported it to me explained. At the time I wondered what had happened to the barrel of salt I had seen Zhora carrying not long before. The Germans took her away. No one mentioned what happened to the soup.

An old woman who had lived down the street and never spoken to us before started hanging around. We still had the bag of experimental fodder that my father had brought home when his college closed. It contained some alfalfa and tasted bitter. It looked like powdered rodent food. My mother made buns out of it and gave each of us one every day. At first repulsive, these soon became edible, and then delicious. The old woman would sit in a corner and watch us eat. Her eyes would water, her lips would move, she would drool like one of Pavlov's dogs.

One day she walked up to me and digging her fingers into my arm said, "You are such a pretty little boy, and you have some meat on your bones, and you are fat in some places, too."

My father started slapping her and drove her out the door. "Go out and die, you old bitch, and stop bothering us!" he yelled. My mother, ever the liberal, pleaded with him. "Please, Vassia, she's old, she's hungry, she doesn't mean it." So the old woman was driven out, but after the manner of old women, she got her revenge. We found her dead, across our front stoop, two mornings later. My father dragged her down the street where she was soon covered by snow.

By now we had entered the depth of Russian winter. The snow was crisp and icy. Touching a metal object with a naked hand would lead to the skin freezing to the metal. Withdrawing the hand meant leaving the skin behind. At the nearby front, soldiers' hands froze to their rifles, mittens and all.

Since we were near the front lines, the city remained under army control instead of the civil administration. The army was rather busy fighting a war under arctic conditions with very little winter equipment. Their machines would not work, their soldiers froze, their transport could not move. I doubt they would have been able to do anything for the civilians even had their peculiar racial doctrine permitted it.

To the German Army, we were troublesome vermin that infested places of tactical interest and had to be swatted now and then. These nows and thens became ever more frequent as the Soviets began to parachute special teams behind the German lines to kill Germans, who, true to their word, would then hang ten hostages for each of their killed soldiers. I attended one such hanging.

Russian architects appear to have been inordinately fond of balconies. Every multistoried building was festooned with them.

Every balcony had an iron railing. It was from these railings that the telephone cable nooses had been suspended. Since electricity was out and there was no coal, all centrally heated buildings were covered with a thick layer of ice. They sparkled in the sun like ice-palaces. Everything was very white except for the black-clad spectators and green-uniformed Germans.

First, an interpreter in a German uniform came out on the balcony and read a proclamation, first in German, then in Russian. These interpreters were some of the slimier subspecies uncovered by the war. They were mostly Volga Germans or Balts. Where the Germans, superior in their self-concept, merely held us in contempt and disdain, the interpreters had personal scores to settle with the Russians. They not only hated us but were also venal and corrupt. Due to their dialectic straightjackets, the Germans were capable only of a limited number of reactions. They were as predictable in these as any Marxist theoretician. By choosing what to interpret or what nuance to inject into their interpreting, the interpreters could effectively manipulate the actions of their masters. This they constantly did to their enrichment and gratification.

As can be expected, they were not held in high regard by anyone. The one on the balcony that day read the reason for which the men were to die and admonished us not to cut down the corpses for 24 hours. Then the men were led out and hanged one at a time. All but one moved with a wooden resignation. Nooses were placed around their necks, a sergeant adjusted the knots, and they were pushed off the balcony. They didn't twitch much.

Except for one individualist among them, the affair would have been mundane. The one exception was not about to submit to his fate without a struggle. He pleaded. He cried. He dropped on his knees in front of the German. When the German kicked him off the balcony, he managed to grab the edge of it and hang on, screaming all the while. The German stomped on the man's fingers with his hobnailed boots, and the man fell to swing beside his companions. The German who had done the stomping looked self-conscious, embarrassed by the sloppiness of the operation, no doubt.

In spite of the German's admonition, the corpses were all gone by the next morning, and some shockingly pink hamburger was being sold under the guise of dog or cat meat. Everyone knew, and everyone pretended not to know. One day my mother fed us some on our alfalfa buns. It was the most delicious stuff I had ever tasted. I have felt guilty about it ever since.

That winter we could tell who had died by looking at their windows. As long as there was life, there were melted patches on the glass. As soon as the window became coated with a thick sheet of ice that remained for several days, we knew the people inside had died.

I saw Marussia for the next to the last time about a month before the hanging. I was standing by an old storage shed that had large, skeletal patches where boards had been pried off for firewood. I was munching on my daily alfalfa bun with some distaste, that being before they became delicious. Marussia walked up to me looking like a blonde teddy bear in a blue overcoat. "Do you want to see my pussy?" she asked. I nodded. "Then give me a bite," she demanded.

Thus in all innocence, she became a prostitute while wolfing down the rest of my bun, and I became a john. Perhaps not, though, because halfway through her trying to pull up her coat she stopped.

"I am very tired," she said. "Mother says we will both go to sleep soon, and then when we wake up everything will be like before the war and there will be lots to eat. I will pay you back for the bun then."

"Are you eight yet?" I asked for lack of anything better.

"I am," she said. We stared across the river at the burned out tractor factory. "I better go home now. It's time for my nap. Mother says the more I sleep, the less I'll be hungry." I walked her to her stairs; she stumbled a little.

I had all but forgotten her in the events that followed. Life was quite unpredictable, and each day brought with it something new and unexpected.

One day my father went to work for the Germans. They were organizing a research lab to increase crop production in the Eastern

Territories (*Ostgebiet*), and ship food back to Germany. He went away that morning and came back carrying a bag of rations. They had given him sausage skins and sweepings off the floor of a grain storage bin. That was his pay as a scientist. It was also life.

My mother fixed multigrain, sausage-skin soup, and the four of us sat down to eat.

"We will be leaving the city," my father said. "The Germans will be centralizing the research station further west. We are too near the front here."

After the meal, I went into the yard to play. I was feeling good. Life had stopped being a chancy business and had become an iron certainty again. I was immortal. I ignored the dark objects jutting from the snowdrifts. I was looking forward to travel and excitement. I looked around the huge yard, already saying goodbye to the things of childhood.

The trench we had been hiding in when the bridge was blown up was covered in snow, creating a soft, inviting ridge. The doors leading into it were open. I had been forbidden by my parents to go near it, but this was special. I was soon to leave. I peered into it. It was dark, cold, and slightly mysterious. I entered and let my eyes adjust to the dim light.

It was like a reunion or an unexpected party when old friends show up. There they were, wrapped and partly unwrapped. Pieces of them were missing, but all the heads were there. The policeman's wife had a large black split in her forehead. Some old woman was unrecognizable in a mass of wrinkles and ice. And there was Marussia. She was very blonde. Her lips were slightly open, and her front teeth could be seen. Her eyes were ice. There was so very little of her left inside her wrappings.

I left the trench and went home. I had grown up for the first, but far from the last, time in my life.

3

We departed Kharkov on February 2, 1942, leaving our apartment unlocked so our neighbors could utilize my parents' extensive library for fuel. Packing a few belongings on three children's sleds, we set out for the rail station about two kilometers distant. I distinctly recall pulling a sled on which my three-year-old brother was sitting, looking cute in a gray fur coat. My father was pulling a sled in front of me; my mother, the one behind. Both were keeping an eye out for persons who might snatch my brother or me for the evening meal. The street was lined with burned, bombed-out buildings. An occasional black limb stuck out of the snow drifts along the way, as if in farewell or derision. It was a relief to reach the station.

The Germans provided us with German Army rations for one week. This was paradise. We went trooping into a passenger coach full of German soldiers. One of them looked up briefly to say, "Russen raus!" and went back to his game of Twenty-One. Somewhat crestfallen, we wound up in a cattle car full of our own kind.

The cattle car was gloomy and quiet. Straw and horseshit covered the floor. The people huddled in small groups, conversing in whispers. Since ordinary civilians could not travel, these were collaborators of various sorts and black market dealers. Oppressed by a knowledge of their crimes against their own and their low status among the Germans, they sat amidst guilt and horseshit. The train started, stopped, and started again, and it finally settled into a slow and steady speed. I spent some time staring out the one tiny window at the world. Russian winter landscapes tend to be drab and pedestrian at the best of times. In wartime, with the added wreckage, they are profoundly depressing. I sat down with my family and fell asleep.

Sleep was far more than rest. It was an escape. To this day, I find myself enjoying it more intensely at stressful times. So I was quite irritated by my parents waking me up every two hours or so and asking me to jump around and wave my arms. Evidently they considered this to be a cure against frostbite. I would jump about if the train wasn't jolting too much at the time, ask my parents if that was enough jumping, and go back to sleep or to looking out the one small window.

Once I saw a field full of dead horses. They lay in rows with rearing heads, twisted necks, and extended haunches and legs sticking out of the snow. Someone said they were the remnants of a Soviet cavalry charge against the Germans. I wondered if the men were also out there covered by snow, or if someone had gone to the trouble of burying them.

At times we would pass knocked-out German tanks. The tanks were always opposite a Soviet anti-tank gun. They were mostly the small Pzkw II types with two short, thin barrels sticking out of the turret. They were either painted red as some form of memorial or had turned red when they had burned.

We frequently passed the wreckage of Soviet trains by the side of the embankment. Many of these had been Red Cross trains with the emblems still clearly visible. There was no shortage of depressing stuff to look at. I would stare at it, go to sleep, and be woken up to jump around, stare at it all some more. The trip was rather uneventful.

We were supposedly going to Kiev, the one-time capital of Ukraine, established in the ninth century by Viking princes. Normally it was a 24-hour rail trip. Due to blown up bridges and the fact that military rail traffic had priority, it took us three weeks to reach it. We spent one of these weeks sitting in the dreary little town of Kremenchug. We stayed with a family whose son would go out to a frozen lake every day to fish. My father and I would go with him. The kid would chop holes through the ice in spots known to him and catch tiny perch. As a favor for us, he would pull out slimy, bivalve mollusks such as can be found in any river or lake. We would make truly repulsive soup out of them.

When our train got going again, it seemed a miracle. We next wound up in Poltava, a small town near Kiev, where Peter the Great defeated the combined armies of Charles the XIIth of Sweden and a Ukrainian Cossack Army. That was in the eighteenth century, and for the first time, Ukraine became a part of Russia.

After defeating the Swedes, Peter buried them all in a mass grave and put up a handsome monument to "Swedish warriors who bravely perished in battle." A lot of Soviet equipment and shot-up transport lay scattered around, and one couldn't help but contrast the military etiquette of the eighteenth century with that of the twentieth.

We stayed for two weeks in a large storage building whose corner had been blown off by a shell. Large rats scurried along the walls, frightening the women, and in a corner, I found a Soviet hand grenade.

On the positive side, we received fresh bread and milk. I had not seen milk since before the war, and its taste surprised me. Four or five women were traveling with our group who were either prostitutes or some other kind of sluts since they wore lipstick. I took to staring at one of them, trying to imagine what her pussy looked like. She quickly became aware of this and would wink at me and say something to her girlfriends, who would break out in loud and raucous laughter.

I hated the coarse bitches and wanted to kill them. I also loved them and wanted to watch them piss and then lick their steaming, hot cunts and fuck them crosseyed. I have sometimes wondered whether this is a normal developmental stage for an eight-year-old. I would wind up ramming my hands in my pockets and running away. Neither my attitude nor my method of coping with it has changed significantly in the intervening years, but now I conceal it better.

During Operation Barbarossa, a very large part of the Soviet Army had been encircled around Kiev and had fought for several weeks. Equipment was scattered far and wide, too much for the Germans or anyone else to pick up within a reasonable length of time.

A group of four trucks had been abandoned near our building. Every time I felt humiliated by my lust/hate objects, I explored the trucks. One of them had a large square tank on its back with small rings sticking out along the side. Twisting and pulling on the rings made it possible to withdraw a long, highly polished metal rod coated with thick grease. The rod had a numbered scale running along its length. Unaware of the obvious Freudian connotation, I would slide the rod in and out of its greasy home until my self-confidence returned and I could go back to observing these women.

There is something infinitely desirable about women. Men (at least at certain times in our lives) long for it. We would kill for them, and, would readily die for them. Yet upon closer approach and inspection, the feeling dissipates, and all we get is sex and love. After a number of girlfriends and wives, our initial lust declines, leaving us with the ability to truly get along with women.

But back in 1942, when I was eight years old, there were only immediate and powerful forces in my life. Terror, hunger, and (I am glad to say) lust shaped my days. An awareness of things unknown also allowed the possibility of the miraculous. I miss it today.

After two weeks in Poltava, we were able to catch a train to Kiev. All I remember of this ancient and supposedly beautiful city are snowdrifts, blocks of ruins that were bombed by the Germans or blown up by the retreating Russians, and German sentries in huge straw overshoes. It was bitterly cold.

My father had to remain in Kiev since his German research laboratory was located there, so he sent us to his ancestral village, Chizincy, near Medvin.

In my view, mankind has passed the apex of its cultural development and has begun the ever-accelerating slide towards its juncture with the dinosaurs. It is a pity that we will take so many other species with us, but provided we do truly become extinct, it will be worth the price.

Still, I may be wrong. An amazing spiritual renaissance may come about, and we may yet escape statistical probability and live up to our potential. If this occurs, and if the scientific marvels predicted by science fiction are realized, we may discover time travel. Should we do this, I am certain that the explorers going back to a Stone Age agricultural community will find conditions practically identical to those I found in my father's village in the summer of 1942.

The village consisted of a random scattering of mud huts with straw roofs. There was no electricity. There was no running water. There weren't even any outhouses. The peasants went out "behind the hut" and found a handy bush. In the entire village, there were only two wells, and one had to go to one to draw water and bring it back in two buckets typically carried on opposite ends of a wooden yoke that fit about one's neck and shoulders. There was a large collective farm on which the peasants worked. Each family was allowed a cow or a horse and could also keep one pig. They were also allowed a small strip of land, about half an acre, to grow vegetables for themselves.

The government took the produce from the collective farms. Before the war it had been the Soviet government; now it was the Germans. The issue of land ownership was the only issue of interest to the peasants. They were anti-Communist because the Communists had taken away their land and by the establishment of the collective farms had created a neo-feudal society. Had the Germans returned the land, they would have had total support and probably would have won the war. But to the Germans, we were *Untermenschen*, a mass of sub-humanity. Our fate was a matter of total indifference to them.

Being a city boy, I was shocked by the conditions and by the incredible ignorance of just about everyone. They in turn regarded me with much suspicion.

The village was organized into two mutually suspicious societies, one male and the other female. There was not very much contact between the two except, presumably, in bed. From earliest childhood, boys played with and related to other boys, and girls passed from a playful, romantic girlhood to a nasty, overworked femininity within their own social circle. Boys my age herded horses in the surrounding steppe. They rode the animals bareback and jumped them over ravines. A significant number of the boys became crippled from these activities.

The girls herded cows and lay around, making garlands and fantasizing about a future marriage. Upon reaching the age of sixteen, the fate of both sexes was to work at the collective farm, which rapidly turned them into overworked, wrinkled old people.

I quietly observed this situation and decided to herd cows with the girls. The village was astounded. No such thing had ever happened before. Old Cossacks would look at me as I walked by and scratch their heads. My father's family was scandalized. They had a well-deserved reputation for homicidal rages and random mayhem that was put in serious jeopardy by my decision. Two of the boys started giving me a hard time, so I picked up a piece of firewood and laid one of them out colder than shit. The other one ran off with a bloody nose. This action restored my family's reputation, and I was left alone to pursue my heterosexual activities among the cowgirls.

In the many years that have passed, I have frequently wished that I had had the anthropological training of a Margaret Meade since the group I had observed was surely as primitive as anything to be found in Samoa.

Although the Soviets had gotten rid of all religion and all priests in the 1930s, the girls were not only religious, but superstitious as well. They believed in witches and practiced pagan rituals. In spite of exhibiting themselves to me sexually, they were all virgins and determined to remain such until their marriages. In fact, their chances of getting married would have been nil had they not been virgins. This, combined with their state of virtually nonexistent cleanliness and having fleas, lice, and worms, made the thought of any sexual activity repulsive. All that was left was visual gratification and lots of dirty talk.

And so the summer passed. I spent my days staring at young pussies and engaging in coarse sexual conversations. Nights were spent in bed with my twelve-year-old cousin, Raya, and my kid brother. We scratched flea bites, and she handled my prick, which refused to get hard. On Sundays, we sat in the sun, and my mother combed lice out of our heads with a fine-tooth comb.

My father's family consisted of his sister, Catherine, a shrunken and worn-out slattern who had been abandoned by her husband, her twelve-year-old daughter, Raya—blonde, dirty minded, and determined to retain her virginity—and an old, wizened grandmother. There had once been a grandfather who had shot a priest who had unsuccessfully prayed for rain. The same grandfather had reputedly impregnated a sixteen-year-old shortly before his death at the age of ninety.

There had also once been an Uncle Ivan, who during the Revolution had recruited his own "army," proclaimed his own "republic," and had then proceeded to emulate the world governments by stealing everything that did not move under its own power and raping everything that did. When it became obvious that the Communists were going to win, Uncle Ivan took his "army" over to them and was rewarded after the Civil War by being made a forest ranger/game warden. He took his new position as seriously as he had taken the leadership of his "army." It is customary in that part of Ukraine for village women to pick up fallen twigs in the forest for firewood. Uncle Ivan set out to apprehend as many of these "enemies of the people" as he could and punish them on the spot by raping them. He was finally transferred to the Far East, where forests are vast and women are few.

My mother, having a PhD. in literature and the humanities, did not take well to our bucolic idyll. She kept taking me aside and telling me that the peasants were ignorant, dirty, and uneducated and that I should not play with them. If she had only known! She finally got into a horrid screaming row with Aunt Catherine, so we hired a horse cart and were driven to the small town of Bohuslav where yet another relative awaited.

That summer in the village stands out in my memory not only as an experience outside all known time and civilization, but also as a holiday from the war. I later learned that during their retreat, the Germans burned the village and wiped out its occupants. According to Wehrmacht archives, the SS division "Wiking" together with an independent heavy tank battalion and infantry units attacked the village in February of 1944. They did this to free some encircled German units. My stone age relatives just happened to be in the way. I don't blame the Germans a bit.

Bohuslav literally translated means "Praise the Lord." My first evening there I went wading in a nearby river. It was October, and ice was forming near the bank. I promptly came down with a cold, which turned into pneumonia. Laid up for months with a severe fever, I was not expected to live.

We were staying with a great-aunt who was a practicing witch. Peasant women walked for miles through sleet and snow to seek her services. They paid in chickens and produce. She cast spells to keep husbands from straying or to retrieve those who had strayed. She made love potions. She communicated with the departed, of whom by this time there were many. She concocted a potion to make an old woman's husband impotent. Once she cast a spell to dry up someone's milk. I never found out whether this someone was human or bovine. Like all the other peasant women I had met that summer, the great-aunt was also dirty minded in the extreme. When my mother had gone out, we would have some notable conversations that always ended with the admonition "…don't tell your mother. She is a fine woman, God bless her, but she is educated and would not understand."

At this time, I was trying to read Boccaccio's *The Decameron* and finding it heavy going. The aunt kept snatching it from me and handing me the *Lives of the Saints* instead. I wish I remembered more of the *Saints* for in its own way it was a volume far more wondrous and kinky than Boccaccio's. One evening the aunt cast my fortune and told me that far from dying, as I was expected to do, I would live to a very old age and "…fuck many women, though you will never get the one you really love." Oh well, what is real love? Most people would disagree on that subject just as most would agree on what constitutes a wicked fuck.

It was here that the war caught up with us again. First, a Hungarian division spent a week quartered in the town. A Ukrainian SS division then replaced it. This in turn moved on and gave its place to a German Wehrmacht unit. Of all these troops, the Hungarians were by far the most humane and civilized. To this day, I retain a friendly feeling towards Hungarians based on my wartime exposure.

The spring of 1943 arrived, and I recovered. So apparently did the Soviet Army. They began an offensive that threw the Germans out of thousands of miles of territory. Since we had somehow cast our lot with the Germans, we had to leave.

4

We left Bohuslav in a horse cart. When I think back on our journey, I can only compare traveling by horse cart across the steppe to sailing on the San Francisco Bay. It had that same sense of being part of a natural rhythm. The creaking of the rigging, the sounds of the boat, and the action of wind and wave are strangely analogous to the creaking of the horse cart, the gentle undulation of the steppe, and the quiet plodding of the horse, interrupted by an occasional fart and swishing of the whip.

We first drove down a very rutted and muddy track that led alongside a paved road. There was heavy traffic along the road. German trucks loaded with troops, command cars, motorcycles, and an occasional halftrack full of helmeted troops went to the east. An occasional truck and a few ambulances went the other way.

The cart driver and my mother promptly got into a long, monotonous conversation aimed at discovering a mutual ancestor. They managed to locate several common acquaintances and gossiped about each one in great detail. My brother and I soon fell asleep.

The chill of the evening woke me up. The cart was stopped on a rise, and, looking towards the east we could see a large number of pink splotches on the horizon. The cart driver cursed in a monotone while my mother remained silent.

"Fucking Germans. Look at the bastards. Coming here and hanging people and burning villages. I can see them hanging somebody that fights them, but what the fuck do they have to burn the villages for and drive people away?" muttered the driver. We sat and watched while the pink sky turned alternatively brighter and darker again. Then the driver cracked his whip, and we drove on.

Eventually, we arrived at another small town called Bila Tserkva (White Church). We stayed at the house of yet another relative. One of my profligate uncles was also visiting, accompanied by a large, giggly woman. In retrospect, Uncle George was fucking a real pig.

We stayed for only a couple of weeks. A Hungarian unit occupied the town, and the cheerful, humane Hungarian soldiers were a pleasant contrast to the Germans. We stayed near an old Red Army barracks that had been destroyed by the retreating Russians. It had been used by an anti-aircraft unit. The unit had abandoned many of its guns, which were large, unwieldy, rapid-fire cannons. Judging by the numerous expended shell casings surrounding them, they were somewhere between 25-30 mm in caliber.

Several Ukrainian and Russian units in the neighborhood were training to fight alongside the Germans. They were being trained by German non-commissioned officers wearing nickel-plated bayonets with staghorn handles and tassels. The Ukrainians had been issued old Red Army uniforms and boots. The Russians still wore their civilian clothes. Both Russians and Ukrainians were armed with Soviet "three-line" rifles.

One day I was walking past a Russian unit that occupied a long trench preparatory to jumping out and running a mock attack. I was carrying several large cigarette boxes in which I had started a butterfly collection. One of the Russians jumped out of the trench and tore the boxes out of my hands, under the impression that they contained cigarettes. He was quite unhappy with the discovery of my butterfly collection and threw the boxes at me, yelling at me to "get the fuck out of here before I fuck you up your ass!" I promptly got the fuck out of there. I had learned a lesson about tobacco addiction that I was to find quite valuable a few years later.

Not very long after this incident we were loaded on an old Soviet truck and taken to the town of Uman where we rejoined my father, whose German-serving laboratory had moved there before its evacuation to Germany.

Uman was the last place we lived in the USSR. There was a large German airfield nearby. Huge six-engined transports took off and landed continuously. They had corrugated bodies that looked a little like Nissen huts and tracked landing gear.

There was also a nearby lake inhabited by perch, crawfish, and numerous frogs. I quickly made friends with the local urchins, who taught me how to catch crawfish and blow up frogs. One took a grass stem, inserted it into the hapless amphibian's asshole, and blew into it rather hard. The frog swelled up like a blimp and, when thrown back into the lake, skittered along the surface unable to dive. For some reason, we found this wildly amusing.

One day a German motorized unit arrived in a cloud of dust. The trucks and halftracks were painted in mottled camouflage, the first such paint job I had ever seen. The soldiers were quartered among the civilian population. "Our" German turned out to be a rather sweet, terribly idealistic, and very cute nineteen-year-old named Heinrich. The very first day, he started sharing his rations with us. I had never met a truly kind person before. At least, not a male one. Our men were far more macho, and their kindness was of a gruff, off the cuff variety.

Heinrich made quite an impression on all of us. He was in a Luftwaffe ground unit, which no doubt accounted for his having retained his gentleness and idealism. He would not have lasted long in a combat unit. However, he did not lack courage or convictions. Decades later, I discovered that while he was a member of the Luftwaffe on the Eastern Front, he had written his father, a devout Nazi, a letter in which he stated, "I do not believe in this war, and I do not like this war." Had a censor caught that it would have had dire consequences.

Heinrich and my mother became the best of friends. My father worked at the lab and didn't get home until late. Heinrich usually had duty during normal working hours. He got over an hour off for lunch. Years later, when I was with the US paratroops, I realized what a truly pussy service Heinrich had been in. He gave my mother his address in civilian life, and they somehow managed to stay in touch through all the chaos that followed.

In 1974 while on sabbatical leave, I visited him in northern Germany. He had a corpulent wife and three children. They were pacifists and vegetarians. I was invited to share an inedible lunch of indigestible plant matter. We sat around in a circle, holding hands, chanting messages of peace and goodwill. That evening I invited them out to dinner at a decent restaurant. They forgot about vegetarianism and pigged out on steaks. So Heinrich was a true German after all.

Back to the war. One night we heard the typical rattle of a Soviet aircraft. We went outside. Dull yellow flares hung in the cloudy sky. The plane circled for hours, dropped two small bombs, and flew away.

This scenario was repeated every night from then on. The Russians did no damage but simply kept everyone up. It was more annoying than frightening and certainly not to be compared to the incredible bombing raids unleashed on Germany by the British and the Americans.

It started to rain. All the roads turned into rivers of mud and motorized traffic ground to a halt. I watched a dozen Germans pushing for over an hour to get a command car a hundred yards down the road. Somehow, in spite of the mud, the war ground closer. One day it snowed, and the ground froze. Movement became possible. We sat and watched trucks full of grim Germans driving towards the front. Most of the trucks were towing anti-tank guns, and the Germans looked desperately unhappy.

Soon it was Christmas time. We sat around a smoking stove most of the time. Heinrich's unit pulled out. Before he left, he and my mother had a long, sad conversation. I followed him like a bereft puppy to the street, where he threw his pack and rifle into the back of a truck. He climbed in after them and was driven away.

I stood and listened to the sounds of the truck dying away in the distance. When they had almost dissipated in the air, I thought I heard them grow louder again. I felt the merest hint of some sort of vibration. I stood and listened, desperately trying to bring back first the sound of the truck, then the truck itself, and finally Heinrich. The truck did not reappear, but the faint vibration remained. Late that evening, I went out to listen again. The vibration had become more definite and uneven. It was distant artillery fire.

The next day my father was told that we had to leave. We spent the day frantically packing our few suitcases and tying our other belongings into bundles. The artillery fire came closer. I ran around, saying good-bye to my friends. They had suddenly stopped being friendly. I was leaving with the Germans. I was a traitor.

That evening a truck drove up, and we hurriedly threw our stuff in the back and climbed in. There were three other families in there already. We were driven to the railway station and saw the familiar straw-strewn cattle cars. This time we were to have an armed escort. Just like that, we turned from collaborators into prisoners.

At the precise moment that a guard in a greatcoat entered our car, sat down in the straw, and leaned his rifle against the wall, I permanently divorced myself from my parents. I had followed them through their pointless travels around the countryside. I had tried to do as I was told. I had trusted them and their leadership. Now they had led me here. I knew what happened to people in guarded cattle cars. And I swore to myself that should I survive this latest adventure, I was never, ever going to trust them or follow them again.

All this time the artillery fire had been drawing closer. It was now so close that one could clearly feel the shockwaves passing through the air. The train started and slowly pulled us out of Uman and into the snow. It was slow going. We kept stopping at various sidings to allow military trains to get by. And all the time the artillery fire continued.

At one station we were stopped next to a German canteen train. The fat sergeant who appeared to be in charge of the car directly across from ours gave me and my brother a piece of hard candy. His train had been there for two days, but he was not particularly perturbed by it. This helped to settle my nerves somewhat. The whole time, I had expected to be overtaken by a Soviet tank column and to be shot for treason. Being shot for treason appeared to be the favorite topic of conversation among the losers in our cattle car. They sat in their dark corners on the filthy straw and muttered to each other about it. Their wives bitched at them about it. Sometimes the bitching got quite vicious, and then there would be the sound of a slap and either a howl or quiet, hysterical weeping.

In the middle of all this, a youngish couple sat quietly holding hands. The woman was horribly pregnant. While all the stress, filth, poor nutrition, and shapeless winter clothing combined to make all the women look far from their best, this girl was truly ugly, with a kind of hapless, pathetic ugliness that is as feminine as true beauty. Whenever I got tired of staring at the endless snow, my eyes kept returning to her hunched body, pinched face, and wide, helpless eyes. She and her husband must have been truly in love. There was no other explanation for their being together.

At one of our frequent stops, we found ourselves next to a German armored train. Square living-quarter cars were interspersed with lower cars that bore great octagonal turrets. Protruding from these were short barrels of about six- to eight-inch caliber. There was also a flat car with a Mark III tank. The entire train had been painted white. The turrets bore black crosses.

We were allowed to leave our train to stretch. Not many of us did, due to the bitter cold. I jumped around from one foot to the other to keep from freezing. In the middle of this, I suddenly noticed a rifle cartridge under the armored train. It had a dark green, lacquered steel case with a beautifully streamlined black bullet protruding from it. I badly wanted to pick it up but was afraid of sticking my arm under the wheels of the train to get it. No starving beggar in front of a bakery or a jewel thief in front of a jewelry case could have felt the degree of lustful desire I felt for that cartridge. Even today, fifty years later, I still wonder what it would have been like to have reached out and grabbed it. To have possessed for a short time its sleek, deadly beauty.

My lustful dreams about ordnance were interrupted by the shouting of our guards. We got back on the train, which started to move slowly. The turrets of the armored train began to glide by us. Suddenly long, white flames shot out of the short barrels with a sound like a thunder clap. Dust and straw whirled up from the floor of our car. Before the guard rolled the door shut, I saw a perfect smoke ring in the pink morning sky slowly dissolving above the pink-tinged armored turrets.

There were more shots as our train gathered speed, and the ugly girl began to give birth.

My parents promptly made me look away lest I, God forbid, catch sight of the ugly girl's cunt and be morally warped for life. Looking away from anything is a tedious and boring occupation. I tried it for a while and then went to sleep. It was hard going, what with the ugly girl's animal noises, but by concentrating on the sound of the train wheels, I managed to do it. A new and different sound woke me. It was thin, reedy, piercing, and as ugly in its way as was the ugly girl in hers.

From that moment on, hating the newborn child completely preoccupied me. It cried often and always at the wrong time. Its crying and my trying to sleep appeared to be causally related. We had finally outdistanced the artillery fire, and the trip settled down into boring drudgery. It was bitterly cold. Icy drafts penetrated the cattle car. By cowering behind our bundles, I was able to find a spot out of the draft, and in spite of my parents' efforts to keep me awake and jumping around periodically to forestall frostbite, I tried to sleep. I would close my eyes, and the damned child would start its thin, piercing wail. The only positive feature of the entire squalid episode was that now we did not have to look at the ugly girl's face. She spent every moment bent over her child, making small noises at it. She stayed awake for several days, and, having exhausted herself, eventually fell asleep. The infant cried and wailed and finally fell quiet. It had wet itself and frozen solid. No one bothered to wake either of the parents.

When the mother woke up, she first did some serious screaming, and then she tore up her husband's face for not having watched over the child. Then she collapsed in a sobbing heap, clutching the tiny corpse and talking to it.

Meanwhile, the other adults in the cattle car, good scientists and liberals all, stared at her and muttered. Words like "decomposition," "unsanitary," and "epidemic" were thrown around. Finally, several of them formed a committee and started talking to the ugly girl and her husband. The husband appeared indecisive, but the ugly girl would have none of it. She backed up against the wall of the car and clutched her baby. Her face, twisted by emotion and covered by tears, looked uglier than ever. Eventually, two men held her shoulders while her husband pried the baby out of her hands and handed it to one of the other members of the committee. The guard opened the door, there was an icy blast of wind, and the infant was gone.

The ugly girl made a horrible moaning noise, far more than a moan. It was truly frightening in a metaphysical way. It sounded like the end of all things. She collapsed slowly, hugged herself, and lay on the floor. Her husband made ineffectual noises and gestures. The wives of the intellectual brigade that had separated the "corpsicle" from its mother now started berating their husbands for having acted in an "uncultured" and inhuman manner.

Two days later, the ugly girl became more active. I could not tell quite what she was saying since I was some distance from her, but it obviously disturbed the people near her. A fresh wave of muttering arose.

All this time the train had been moving, quite slowly, across the unending snowy steppe. Every day the guard would open the door for several minutes to air out the car. He would warn us of the event, and we would bundle up, dreading the cold but needing the fresh air. On this day, the ugly girl turned to her husband and quite loudly said, "I don't blame you, but she needs me. I am her mother," and, before anyone could stop her, jumped out the door and into the snow.

The train was moving at its usual slow pace, and I can still visualize the event with a supernatural, crystalline clarity, much like that induced by psilocybin. The ugly girl landed in the snow. She picked herself up with a puzzled, wide-eyed look. I still see her face clearly against the white landscape, eyes wide open, mouth open with small clouds of frozen breath blowing back against a black coat. She turns around towards the tail of the train and begins to trudge through the snow. Her steps are childlike and unsure. She is holding her arms out for balance. She looks like a large, fat child in her clothes.

The guard works the bolt of his rifle up and down. He aims carefully. The train moves slowly; she is not far away. He cannot miss. The rifle goes off and she falls. The two events are perceived as occurring at the same time. She lies still, without moving, arms held out to her sides in the snow. The train pulls away. The guard closes the door. He does not look happy. In fact, it is obvious that he is quite disturbed.

I can see it any time I want to. All I have to do is close my eyes. Sometimes I can see it when I don't want to, and sometimes I do not have to close my eyes at all. I am still terrified of infants. Whenever they cry, I expect them to stop and die suddenly. I still find ugly, pathetic women rather touching. In my youth, I fucked many of them as a gesture of sympathy and repentance. It resulted in confusion on their part and annoyance on mine. Ugly women know they are ugly. If you show interest in them, they think you are a loser who can't do any better. They despise you for fucking the likes of them and loathe themselves for screwing you. It is not a happy situation. Unless you are ugly yourself, you should leave them alone. Never love an ugly woman. She will not forgive you. But enough of love. Back to the train.

After the guard slammed the door, there was a stunned silence. Then some man said, "So that is what we are to them."

"Oh, shut up," said a woman. "They may shoot you, too."

"He had to shoot; he's a soldier, and he has his orders," said someone else.

"Yes, it's a difficult situation for him, also," added another intellectual. Within ten minutes, these assholes had justified the shooting and successfully distanced themselves from the dead ugly girl. Now she was truly dead.

The husband sat alone on their bundles and sobbed. People kept away from him. Finally, a skinny, horsey lab technician came over and put her arms around him. He sobbed quietly into her shoulder. She led him back to her part of the car where he soon fell asleep. Within a week, they were close friends.

A few days later, we were crossing the Carpathian Mountains. I had never seen mountains before, and I found them not very exciting. I was disappointed to find them covered with trees. I had been expecting cliffs and glaciers.

It had taken us approximately ten days to leave the borders of the USSR and to enter Romania. Romania had not been devastated by the war. There were unbroken windows in the station buildings, and the electric lights worked. We were given a food ration of one large loaf of bread per person and a round cheese per family. The husband of the dead ugly girl and the horsey lab technician now formed a family unit and were treated as such in the distribution of rations. They sat with their arms around each other, munching their bread and cheese.

Romania was just as cold as the Soviet Union had been. The stations were patrolled by soldiers in long, heavy overcoats, carrying short, stubby carbines with brass-handled bayonets. They, like the Hungarians, appeared to be friendlier than the Germans.

We were not long in Romania. The very next day, we were in Hungary. The train was moving faster now; the railway sidings were busier and at the same time far more efficient. I spent most of my time observing the supply trains heading east. There was an incredible variety of stuff being transported. Command cars, stacked on top of each other, were interspersed with tanks and halftracks. The halftracks, in particular, were highly variable. Some bristled with antennae, others had short, stubby howitzer barrels protruding from the front armor plate, and yet others were equipped with long, slender anti-tank guns or multiple anti-aircraft cannons. Truly the world was a fascinating place.

Many of the trains arriving from the east showed signs of partisan activity. They had been machine-gunned low along the sides. The side of the carriage opposite the machine gun looked especially hideous with its splintered bullet holes. I was surprised that the carriage still held together, hadn't in fact torn along some perforated line and fallen apart.

In Hungary, I had my second memorable experience of this journey. It was early morning, and we were stopped at a siding. Suddenly our guard closed the door and barked at us to sit down. There was one tiny window in one corner of the carriage, with an iron grate over it. I had been cultivating the guard, being perfectly aware that soldiers tend to like kids. The guy never smiled back at me, but he would not look at me while delivering some unpleasant order. So now, while the adults sat and sulked, I chanced a quick look through the little window and saw another face looking directly at me out of another such window.

The early morning sun reflected and sparkled on very fresh, very white snow. The boxcar ever so slowly passing mine had icicles hanging from the edge of the roof, and the sun made tiny, multicolored rainbows in them. The iron bars on the window opposite mine had barbed wire wound around them so they could not be grasped. The sun also sparkled on the frost coating the barbs. The face that stared into mine was young and very Semitic, covered with a couple of days growth of beard. The eyes were dark and huge, filled with terminal sorrow. These eyes were filled with tears, and the sun reflected from them, giving them an extraordinary luminosity. The face was aware of me, had classified and dismissed me as insignificant compared to its own mournful self-preoccupation. This face slid slowly past mine, and I ducked back down and sat in my burrow of bundles. The guard had said nothing.

Shortly after this event, we passed Budapest. I saw Buda, and I saw Pest, and I saw the broad, brown Danube. I noticed all the pointed cathedral roofs and all the rounded roofs that so delight the tourists and have some strange significance to historians. I found them neither interesting nor significant.

A few days later, we reached Vienna. Our guard was removed, and we were allowed to see the city for an hour. Since none of us had papers, we walked around in a herd with one of the German officers who administered the research lab and who had traveled in our train in a special Pullman-type carriage. I remember the Prater, a vast and seedy amusement park. I revisited it in 1973 and screwed a kinky, middle-aged whore in leather and garters, in some peculiar and painful ways. In 1944, the place was full of soldiers on leave. They walked around in large groups and appeared rather bored. A mere eight years later, I found out exactly how they felt.

From Vienna, we went to Bruck an der Leitha. It is a small town of great historical and literary significance to those who have read

Hasek's *Good Soldier Schweik*. I had not read it then, but many years later, when I finally did, the book had significantly more meaning for me. I wholeheartedly recommend the book but not the town.

Finally, we reached our destination, which was the small village of Halbturn near the Hungarian border. As we disembarked, another train pulled in. It was loaded with twin-engine Henschel attack planes. The delicate wings of the planes were packed lengthwise along with the fuselages. I admired the camouflage pattern painted on the upper surface of the wings and wished I could touch them but did not dare. We were loaded on several large, rubber-wheeled wagons and pulled by tractors for a couple of miles to an old castle surrounded by a park. This was to be home.

5

Halbturn is a small Austrian village nestled up against the Hungarian border. I revisited it in '74 and was surprised by how small and grubby it was. The streets were unpaved. There were two tavern/restaurants. I had two beers in each, then went for a walk along the border fence. Camouflage uniformed guards stared at me through binoculars from the Communist side. There were no guards on the Austrian side.

I went back to the village, had another beer, and then walked through the estate park to the castle. The castle was in a terrible state of disrepair. I understand that it has now been fixed up and is a tourist attraction. Where my family and dozens of others had been housed, there was now only dust. Both courtyards were filled with fallen leaves. The fountain in the inner courtyard was dry.

I walked the two kilometers to the site of my old labor camp. On the way, I passed a small building in which the lab hunchback had had his lab and nicotine distillery during the war. Doors and windows were missing. The walls were covered with Russian graffiti all dated 1945. It was a sort of monument.

My camp no longer existed. In its place stood a vineyard. I listlessly stared at bunches of green grapes as they reflected the sunlight, not quite sure what to do or feel. After a few moments, I started back for the village. I had trouble walking and discovered to my disgust that I had tears in my eyes. I sat down under a tree to get my mind into operational shape. An Austrian passed on a bicycle and waved. I waved back. Things had certainly changed.

When we arrived in 1944, the castle was in the process of being vacated by some sort of unit that was turning Hitler Youths into SS. They were terribly neat looking and had a very smart guard outside the main gate. Inside, an obstacle course had been set up, and a Hitler Youth was riding a motorcycle through it, around little flags denoting obstacles. In the inner courtyard, a stage was occupied by two kids in boxing gloves beating the shit out of each other. Blood poured out of their noses, but they kept pounding away, observed by their peers.

We were all crowded into one of the buildings for a week. By the end of the week, the Hitler Youth had moved on to some other location, we hoped on the Eastern Front, and we had the castle to ourselves. Living conditions improved somewhat. My family shared a large room, almost a hall, with three other families. For privacy, we strung ropes and hung blankets and sheets to form tent-like walls. As wartime accommodations went, this was pretty good.

We got German ration cards. Suddenly there was food. No one got fat, but no one starved either. Cannibalism became once more an unspeakable perversion. I had nightmares about finding partly cut-up bodies in the snow. My father worked at the lab, my mother cooked, cleaned our area, and gossiped with the other Russian women. There was no school.

I spent my days endlessly roaming the park-like estate. The estate and the castle were owned by an Austrian duke not in residence at the time. The nearby farmers still obviously owed medieval vassalage to him. They always spoke of him with reverence, like God or the Führer.

Towards us, the Austrians displayed implacable hatred and contempt. In all of my travels, I have never found so much prejudice and meanness as in Eastern and Central Europe. When I revisited the place in the '70s, this was replaced by a sickeningly slimy subservience now that I was a "rich" American, but when I was a kid, I seldom passed an Austrian farmer without the latter cursing or spitting on the ground. The ultimate act of petty meanness was displayed by a very old woman who painfully dragged herself across the street to spit on me. I hope when the Red Army took Halbturn, they fucked her to death, but she was so old and ugly even the Russians might have let her go.

In spite of all these petty annoyances, life was good. I kept out of the way of the Germans and spent my days occasionally with two other Russian kids, but usually alone. My brother was now of an age where he wanted to participate in my activities but, being only five years old, his physical endurance was not sufficient to permit this. I usually managed to escape either through stealth or outright bullying.

About this time the village became occupied by a mechanized SS division. Wherever one looked, there were halftracks either parked in front of houses or moving down streets, churning up incredible amounts of dust. One day I was sitting on the steps of a barn that served the village as a weekend movie theater when a halftrack pulled up and stopped. About a dozen troopers came piling out, each carrying a machine gun. They stacked these against the wall, and one of them asked me to keep an eye on the weapons. Then they all went into the barn. I sat on the steps and looked at the guns. They looked lethal as hell, with a dull, oily film on them. I touched one and slid my finger down the cool side of its receiver. Here was the root and the expression of all power. This was the Divine Right of kings, the Popular Will of democracies, the Proletarian Might of Socialist Republics. I lusted after that gun as I have never lusted after a woman. I visualized myself walking down the village street, killing every German I met and then executing over half the Russians in my group.

That gun was the stuff of my childhood dreams. It had a square cooling jacket with oblong cooling slits, a streamlined receiver, and a brown plastic shoulder stock. I now know that it was an MG 42, probably the finest machine gun to come out of the Second World War. Years later, during the Korean debacle, I would stagger through rain and mud carrying a US 1919 A6 Browning. It was square, awkward, temperamental, and heavy. The MG 42 had been altogether a better gun.

But all dreams and great love affairs end. The Germans came out of the barn talking in an agitated manner and munching ration crackers. They took their guns, got into the halftrack, and drove away, leaving me on the steps still dreaming scarlet dreams of slaughtering their civilian population.

The very next day, March 15, 1944, the halftracks formed into a column and drove down the main street to the Hungarian border a couple of hundred meters away. An officer got out of his command car and shot the Hungarian border guard. Then the column drove into Hungary. Germany had just invaded her ally.

The village once more became empty. There was now nothing much to do. There had not been much before the Hungarian invasion, but somehow the absence of the troops had brought home to me just what a desolate jerkwater Halbturn really was.

One day my two friends and I went to the railway station a couple of kilometers away. We waited behind some bushes at a sharp bend in the road until a tractor towing two trailers came by. Then we raced out as the driver slowed for the turn, jumped on the rear fender of the hindmost trailer, and hung on to the upper edge of the loading gate while keeping our heads below it so the driver could not see us in his rearview mirror. We hung on in this rather tortuous manner until in the proximity of the station and then jumped off, completing the journey on foot.

The main attraction of the railway station was that it provided continuity in our lives by keeping us in touch with the war. There were usually munitions trains heading for the Front or trains loaded with wrecked equipment going back to repair depots in Germany. We could stare our fill at tanks, field guns, and halftracks. Even passenger trains had one or more flack cars with a four-barreled 20 mm cannon attached to them.

This day, however, there were no trains. The station lay quiet and hot. We sat around, waiting for a train to arrive. After a while, a station employee came out and chased us away, so we walked a short distance to a small pond. There were four German kids approximately our age swimming at one end of the pond. Giving them a wide berth, we walked completely around the pond and went swimming on the other side. There was a tiny beach there, and after splashing around for a bit, we sat on the bank and talked.

Soon, one of the German kids came swimming over. He walked out of the water, squatted in front of us, and took a shit while staring at us. Then he swam back over to his friends. We sat in silence, staring at the heap of superior German shit.

"Well," I said, "his shit is the same color as ours."

"No," said one of my friends, "it's lighter in color."

We got up and went back to the castle. We never went near the station again.

One morning I heard the deep drone of engines. I looked around but could not see a thing. It sounded as if thousands of airplanes were flying overhead, but strain as I might, I saw nothing. Looking about, I saw others craning their necks. The noise continued for several hours and then stopped.

The same phenomenon occurred the next day, and the day after. Eventually, we became accustomed to it and stopped looking up. One day I chanced to look up and saw faint, tiny white worms crawling across the sky. There were so many of them, I could not believe they were planes. Surely no nation on earth could have so many planes. My friends and I discussed the matter and decided that the planes must be German since they appeared to be unopposed in their migration across German skies.

As time went on, the little white worms descended to lower elevations. Now we could see tiny silver specks in front of the white condensation trails. It became evident that all was not harmonious in the heavenly spheres. Occasionally the sound of engines became frantically disjointed, and one of the silver spots would begin to go up and down as if on a rollercoaster, with its white trail trying to catch up.

Soon after that, a couple of events took place that had a profound impact on my later life. The first was the removal of the pudgy Wehrmacht major who ran my father's research facility. The guy was an obvious goldbrick whose only talent was his limited knowledge of Russian. The rumor was that his scientific credentials were somewhat feeble, and he occupied his administrative position mostly to keep away from more hazardous duties elsewhere. He departed quickly and quietly, leaving behind a haphazardly run lab and a medium-ugly Russian mistress.

His replacement was a grim and silent SS Sturmfuhrer named Von Babow. He had been badly wounded and limped on an artificial leg. He was covered with medals and accompanied by a son of about my age and a small dog. There was no wife, and he shortly took over the previous commandant's mistress. He spoke a ponderous and stilted Russian and scared the shit out of everybody.

His mistress was a doctor of medicine. Doctors occupied the same social level as schoolteachers in Russia. Perhaps this explains why so many of them were women.

So Von Babow's mistress was not held in high esteem by the rest of the lab, quite aside from her sex life. In retrospect, she appears a tall, well put together woman who would have been far more attractive had she not had a mustache. It was the mustache that proved to be the basis for a serious misunderstanding between us.

One day as she was talking to two Russian women while standing next to our previous Commandant, I walked up to her and in all innocence asked about her mustache and whether it interfered with her kissing anyone. There was a small but profound silence, and then the other Russian bitches started hissing at me to apologize and telling me that I was "uncultured." I did not apologize; I simply turned around and ran off. It was one of my rare displays of integrity, and like the others, it was to cost me dearly.

The other event was more serious. One day Von Babow's son came up to me in the courtyard and said hello in Russian. I replied. He then hit me in the face rather hard and ran off. To have hit him back would have resulted in a quick trip to a concentration camp.

I went to see his father. I am certain that in his distinguished career as an SS officer, Von Babow had seen and done just about everything. He certainly looked it. He was a tall, well-built man with graying hair and a grim and implacable face. Yet he managed to look surprised when a skinny eleven-year-old showed up and asked to see him. In his stilted Russian, he asked if my parents had sent me. I explained that my parents were completely unaware of the matter at hand and would in fact not have allowed me to come if they had known. I then explained that his son had struck me in the face and that I considered this to be grossly unfair because I could not hit him back without being sent to a concentration camp.

"Where did you hear about concentration camps? Did your parents tell you that?" asked Von Babow.

"Everybody knows about your concentration camps," I said.

"And you did not strike my son because you were afraid I would send you to a concentration camp?" asked Von Babow. He sent for his son and told us to shake hands. We did this begrudgingly. Then I was dismissed.

The next day I was roaming about the estate as usual when I saw a man on a bicycle, carrying a rifle and wearing a green hat with a hair tassel attached to it. I followed him in hopes he would shoot something. He stopped his bike and called me over. We introduced ourselves. He turned out to be the estate gamekeeper. He had me follow him to a part of the estate I had not frequented before because it was too civilized and inhabited. He had a house there and a rather plump wife. They must have been childless. They made me wash my hands and gave me a piece of poppy seed cake and a glass of milk. They were the first nice Germans I had ever met, aside from Heinrich back in Uman.

When I revisited the place in '74, I was told that the Russians had shot him.

I returned home in a bemused state. Meeting the gamekeeper had given me a great deal to think about. I decided it was too complex to consider each person on their own merits. Such a philosophy was simply unworkable. It was easier, and in the long run more efficient, to calculate a common denominator for a people based on how I perceived the majority of my personal contacts with them. I tried to return to my previous state of pure hatred for the Germans, but a certain ambivalence had crept in.

My parents were highly excited when I got home. My father looked grim, my mother sobbed, and my brother was hiding behind the bed. As usual, my father hit me a few times.

"You are a goddamn idiot who doesn't understand anything," he yelled. "And you have grown too damn big for your age!"

While this was possible, it had never before occasioned this sort of treatment. It took, as usual, a bit more hitting, screaming, and crying until the facts emerged. That morning, while I was meeting the gamekeeper, my father had been summoned by Von Babow and was informed that I would be transferred to a labor camp since

I was big enough to start working for the Reich. Seig Heil! Von Babow's mustachioed girlfriend had been present at the interview.

Just to forestall such an event, my parents had altered my birth certificate, changing the year of my birth from 1933 to 1935 and thereby making me ineligible for forced labor. Von Babow, however, overrode their objections.

(I still have the altered certificate. True to their cultured selves, once the deed was done, my parents were too timid to correct it. As a result, I now have to work two extra years before retirement. But what the hell, I like my job, and should the occasion arise, I can claim to be younger than I am.)

The next morning I took a bag my mother had tearfully packed and climbed into a truck. My father was at work. As we drove out of the courtyard, we passed Von Babow's girlfriend. She smiled.

6

As I attempt to detail the events of long ago, some of them stand out in sharp contrast to the overall dreariness and depression that characterized those years. My arrival at the labor camp in early Fall, 1944, was one such event. I had just turned eleven and felt very grown up.

The camp lay a few kilometers away from the castle at the end of a wide, graveled drive lined with chestnut trees. It consisted of two brick buildings and three barracks. The camp was fenced in, but there were neither guard towers nor a permanent guard at the gate.

I was let in by a shifty-eyed and tough-looking little Russian who evidently was in some position of authority. I was issued an enameled gray bowl, a spoon, and a brown blanket. I was shown my barracks and admonished to get up in time for roll call, not steal, not talk back to any Germans, and to work hard. Then everyone ignored me.

I spent that first day wandering around, exploring the camp, and feeling sorry for myself. I felt, however, a strong sense of elation at being away from my father. I think I am one of the very few people who were actually liberated by the Nazis. Whatever it was that the Germans did to me, it was done by strangers who were enemies, supposedly for lofty patriotic and philosophical reasons. Consequently, it was much easier to accept than the pointless cruelty that had been so freely dispensed at home. Furthermore, whenever I was struck by a German (with the exception of kids), they always had a clear reason for it. I was treated by them much as I used to treat my dogs, except I wasn't fed as well or shown any kindness or given any medical attention.

They did, however, teach me punctuality, diligence, and a sense of responsibility.

Towards noon of that first day, I was told to bring my bowl to one of the brick buildings, which turned out to be the kitchen. There I received a ladleful of potato soup and a slice of black bread. The soup was made from bits and peels of potato that had been boiled for many hours. It was a potato starch sludge with lots of salt added. The bread was very dark, sour, and wet. I can't recall ever having tasted anything so delicious, but probably that was a result of my constant, gnawing hunger.

Every morning we received half a loaf of that bread. In addition, for lunch and dinner, there was a bowlful of some sort of sludge, usually potato soup. On Sundays, we had vegetable soup with actual potatoes and carrots in it and an occasional piece of some sort of animal sinew or gristle. If I spend too much time describing this cuisine, it is because during my stay at that camp, food was my main preoccupation, as it was for everyone else in that place.

Food and terror were the two reins that controlled us. They worked us quite hard on the farms. This outdoor work made us ravenous far beyond our miserly rations. It is not surprising that food, or the lack of it, caused most transgressions and most punishments. We were constantly on the lookout for something to eat, and we ate some rather peculiar things. Thus I learned that taking an ordinary earthworm, drawing it between one's fingers to squeeze all the shit out of it, salting it lightly, and letting it dry in the sun produced an edible item. Knowledge of that sort is not easy to come by, and once gained, is not quickly forgotten.

But on this first day, the newness of it all overwhelmed me, and I had little idea of the labors and rewards that would affect me.

The rest of the crew arrived just around dusk. There were, as I recall, over two dozen of us. I was by far the youngest. Most of the others seemed to have been in their forties, fifties, and maybe even sixties. Perhaps their ratty appearance and my extreme youth made them seem older than they were.

By far, the most unique and disgusting was an old woman who was more than a little insane. She was skinny, filthy, and could not stop talking. Words tumbled from her drool-flecked lips like maggots from a dead cat. She would not complete one word before starting on the next. She sounded a bit like a scooter or moped engine and was, in fact, called Elizabeth Motorcycle.

She was the only one of us interested in something other than food. Her preoccupation, oddly enough, was sex. I can't believe, don't want to believe, someone as hideous as her would have an easy time finding people who would want to screw her. But she seemed to make out all right. Perhaps it is because she was the only woman constantly with us. I am not certain where she was supposed to stay. The Germans, whenever confronted with her, would usually laugh and wave her away. Sometimes, when angry, they would kick her in the ass, and she would stumble away sputtering words and saliva. I don't know whether she was an actual nymphomaniac. I certainly never saw her do anything except straight, missionary-position fucking.

On this, my first, meeting with her, she walked up to me sputtering and spitting and, unbuttoning my fly, stuck her grimy, dry hand inside. My dick, limp though it was, must have recoiled and shrunk to near invisibility. She cackled something derisive and left on some other quest. Some of the men smiled; a couple explained the obvious to me, that Elizabeth was crazy as batshit and not to be taken seriously. I had wondered then, as I wonder now, of what possible significance her life could have been to anyone, including herself.

Almost everyone in the camp smoked heavily. Since there was no cigarette ration, the main preoccupation of these people was to find something to smoke. Thus cigarette butts were worth considerably more than their weight in gold. I saw starving men barter away their bread rations for something to smoke. I saw them break down and cry when someone stole their hoarded tobacco. Probably the only reason I did not see them kill for it was that most of these people were intellectuals and thus had the fighting potential of a herd of guinea pigs.

These people had all survived Stalin's purges. The purges had carried off everyone who had any character whatsoever and thus was able to take any kind of stand. These pathetic people were unable to take themselves seriously, and they disdained everyone else.

They had been conditioned into informing on one another by the Soviet system, so now they sought to gain favor with the Germans through informing. But there was nothing concrete for them to report, and the Germans did not give a rat's ass for ideological differences in their slaves.

Incapable of fighting or any meaningful resistance, the intellectuals turned to acts of petty bitchiness and viciousness. They were made even more pitiful by their moral ugliness. This weakness bred other vices. Aside from being informers, they also stole, lied, gossiped, and hated everything and everyone with a powerless, burning intensity.

Their only claims to humanity and self-respect were their contributions to their professional lives, which were useless and pointless in the present situation. Thus we had a skinny, redheaded doctor of something-or-other who had done some work on Tamerlane's tomb. He kept talking about it. I asked him who Tamerlane was and learned he had been a great leader.

"As great as Hitler or Stalin?" I asked.

Although I did not realize it at the time, my question had put the doctor in a quandary. We were within hearing range of several of his peers, and to have given me a truthful answer would have resulted in his being informed on. He muttered something and moved away.

One abstract and useless activity at which most of the camp residents excelled was chess. The redheaded follower of Tamerlane and a friend of his would lie on bunks on opposite sides of the room and face the walls. Someone would set up a chessboard between them, and either I or another nonplayer would be delegated to move the pieces. Neither player ever turned around throughout the entire game. This normally consumed most of Sunday. Some games went on longer than the day and had to be carried over to the next Sunday. At such times, each player carefully noted down the positions of the pieces and carried the little scrap of paper all week. I could not then understand the point of all that. I could not conceive of desolation so vast that it would send a human being headlong into abstractions in search of escape.

On Sunday, those of us who wished could go to church. The village of Halbturn had a small church located on the park grounds. I no longer remember whether it was Protestant or Catholic. Whichever, it had a high-quality organ, and the guy who played it was also of a high caliber. I would sometimes go listen to the music. On one such occasion, I ran into my family.

We in the camp were required to wear a small rectangular blue and white patch on our jackets that said "OST," meaning "East." We were known as *Ostarbeiter* (Eastern worker), which was a euphemism for slave laborer. Of course, the word slave comes from Slav, as the Germans would point out to us occasionally. Wherever we went, people would look at our OST patches and either keep away or say something mean.

The occasion of running into my family brought all this sharply into focus. Somehow by acquiring the patch, I had lost respectability. My father stared stonily ahead while my mother looked tearfully tragic but did not take a step in my direction. I turned away, and my small group of fellow *Untermenschen* closed protectively around me. We knew we were slaves, and my parents pretended they were not. That was all there was to it.

All this time, the war had been drawing closer. The enemy planes that at first appeared as mere microscopic white worms now flew lower. We could see small silver spots in front of the white lines. Sometimes the planes flew low enough that we could make out four engines.

One day while working in the vineyards, we heard a strange "whop-whop-whop" sound, and looking up we saw a wing come spiraling down towards us. One of the two engines burned brightly, pouring black smoke. There was a white star inside a blue circle on the wing. It crashed amidst a cloud of dust, and one of the propellers went bouncing across the field, eventually sticking with one blade in the earth. Tiny white parachutes hung in the sky. Our guard took off to help capture the flyers. When he returned hours later, he reported that they had been tall, blond, and had chewed on something incessantly.

"It's gum," said our champion chess player. "If they were Americans, they chewed gum. All Americans chew gum."

In Russian, gum and rubber are the same word. Shortly after this event, I managed to obtain a small piece of bicycle inner tube. I went around chewing it for several hours. It left me faintly nauseous but distinctly less hungry.

Another day a large four-engined bomber came flying low overhead. It looked ungainly, had a twin tail with large rounded rudders, and a swollen-looking belly. Four German fighters accompanied it. From time to time, one or the other of the fighters made a pass at the bomber, and the rattle of machine guns could be distinctly heard. I hoped they would shoot it down nearby so I could get a closer look at it, but the sad-looking entourage flew on and disappeared over the horizon.

One sunny day in late summer when we were working in a vineyard spraying copper compound on the grapevines, it began to snow. It was a very warm day, and most of the men (and Elizabeth Motorcycle) had their shirts off. I had just wiped some sweat off my face and was looking up when the sky filled with tiny white dots. There were thousands upon thousands of them. They looked exactly like snow, but when they came down to us, they turned out to be leaflets.

On one side was a cartoon of a grim-looking farmer holding a scythe, standing in a field of grain. The farmer had been labeled "Germany," the field, "Austria." Behind the farmer, his equally grim-looking wife stood gathering grain. The pamphlet contained an article about how great life had been in Austria before the *Anschluss*, which was when the Austrians had elected to join Germany. On the other side of the leaflet were a photograph of a bathing beach and a continuation of the article.

Our *Sturm Abteilung* (SA) guard read one of the leaflets and chuckled. We gathered some of them for toilet paper, but they were printed on high-quality paper that was not well-suited for that purpose. Soon another SA man came along, accompanied by four Hitler Youths carrying large burlap bags. They were gathering up the leaflets. I gave them some of mine, and the SA man smiled and said to the Hitler Youths, "See, he is on our side."

I thought of the burning bomber and the dying bomber that was being attacked by the fighter planes. It seemed stupid to me to send men and planes into such danger to drop silly leaflets. But then, I was only a kid.

One day a formation of bombers flew over, and a plane dropped two bombs on the castle housing my father's lab. They were probably returning from a raid, and the plane had these bombs left over. Both bombs landed in the park surrounding the castle. Both had their tail assemblies torn off by tree branches. Neither bomb exploded.

A gang of men in mustard-colored coveralls arrived. They, too, were under guard. They winched up the bombs and removed the fuse mechanisms when they departed, leaving the bombs lying by the side of the road. One of the bombs had several yellow rings painted around it and bore the letters RDX.

This entire summer, the Germans had been getting progressively meaner and the food rations skimpier. Our potato soup was quite watery now, and the bread had large, glutinous dark chunks of something in it. We ate it all up, of course, and hungered for more.

On one occasion, we had to move some beehives. This gave two of us the opportunity to steal a piece of honeycomb. I stuffed a chunk of it in my mouth, wax, honey and all. Retribution was immediate. I was knocked to the ground by an Austrian farmer. He pulled his boot back for a second or third kick when our guard intervened. I was stood up in front of my fellows and backhanded across the face a few times to the accompaniment of screams of *Russenschwein!* and *Asiatisches Menschentier!* Later, I saw the guard licking some honey off his hand.

This sort of treatment was routine. For serious infractions, one was sent to a concentration camp somewhere around the town of Linz or Salzburg. That camp had something to do with mining, and people sent there were not heard of again.

The severest punishment had to do with German women. We came into contact with farmers' wives regularly. The husbands were getting shot to pieces on the Eastern Front, and the wives were, in many instances, rather horny. But to be caught fucking one of these ladies was tantamount to a death sentence.

Prior to my arrival at the camp, there had been a young man there named Stefan. During my entire sojourn at the camp, people would refer to him sadly, and yet with pride.

"Remember Stefan?" someone would say, and everyone would look smug.

It seems that Stefan had a huge dick and somehow, in spite of the starvation rations, had retained the ability and interest to use it. Maybe his ladies were feeding him in return for services. In any event, Stefan had had something going with two of the women who ran their farms in the absence of their conscripted husbands. The women would call the camp and request him specifically to work. Unfortunately, each became aware of the extent of his labors with the other and turned him in. He was promptly shipped off to Linz.

Stefan was mostly remembered with disdain by the Russians, since they have a tendency towards prudishness and a Victorian morality that is strangely at odds with their lifestyle. But there was also a certain satisfaction in knowing that at least one of us had done something to one of them.

One day a Waffen SS division arrived and took up residence in the village and the castle. They appeared rather battle weary and had been retreating all the way from the Black Sea. Their transport was all horse drawn, and they also had some camels they had captured during their long-ago advance, and which they now used for transport. The camels were large brownish-gray beasts with two humps. They looked rather exotic in the Austrian setting.

The main contribution of this new group of arrivals was a spectacular military funeral. One of their members, during their second day's stay, had an accident with a panzerfaust launch tube and had blown a large hole through his chest.

The panzerfaust was one of the more fearsome anti-tank weapons of the war. It looked like a giant sperm with its tail held out straight behind it. The head of the sperm was blunted in front and about six inches in diameter. The tail of the sperm was a launch tube containing a powder charge and a sight-trigger box attached to the outside. When the trigger was activated, the head went flying off at the same time a long flame shot out the back of the launch tube. The head was accurate to about fifty meters. It would go through any tank armor of the period (or, more accurately, it would shoot a stream of molten metal into the tank by using an inverted cone principle). Anyone standing within fifteen or so meters of the back of the launch tube would be injured by the back-blast.

The SS gave this man a funeral that was a model of precision and showmanship. The entire village, my entire camp, and my father's lab were in attendance, as well as the entire infantry division. The honor guard was immaculately turned out. I have never seen shinier boots in my life, not even during my later service in the US Army paratroops, where we prided ourselves on the splendor and luster of our jump boots. There were two ministers in attendance: the village pastor and the SS chaplain. The service lasted about 30 minutes, and then the honor guard came goose-stepping up to the grave. Three volleys were fired, each sounding like one shot, and the show was over. The troops marched back to their billets, the villagers went home, and we went back to work.

Around this time, the Austrian duke who owned the estate of which the castle was a part made his appearance. He was a balding, middle-aged man who looked rather inoffensive. While he was there, he staged a hunt for all the officers of the SS division. All the local peasants and we *Untermenschen* got to participate. We were told to pick up a couple of sticks and line up across the entire width of the estate. We then slowly walked forward, hitting the sticks against each other or any nearby trees. This drove all wildlife in front of us and towards the waiting hunters.

It was all incredibly medieval, the subservience of the peasants and their adoration of their ancestral duke, the class difference between the SS officers (descendants of the Germanic knights?) and the peasants, and finally us, the bottom dregs of humanity. Following the hunt, the duke threw an all-night party for the officers, the goal of which was to drink his wine cellars dry before the Russians got them. He then escaped to Argentina, and the officers died for their Führer. A happy ending for all, and an appropriate one.

Two nights after the hunt, we were awakened by the dry rattle of a Soviet airplane engine. We went outside. Smoky yellow flares hung in the murky sky. The plane, of course, could not be seen. It went around and around, dropped a small bomb that exploded harmlessly in a field, and was replaced by another plane that did the same thing. Our people had caught up with us.

In another week's time, the SS division went away to die by a large Hungarian lake in a futile counter-offensive. They were buried in hastily scraped-out mass graves without any honor guards whatsoever. A Luftwaffe 88 battery briefly replaced them. The battery was very shiny and new. The guns were new. The men were new. The tracked prime movers for the guns looked like they had just left the factory. The guns were parked neatly in the village square and inspected daily along with their crews by a group of shined and polished officers. The Soviet planes continued to come over every night, but the battery took no action against them. They stole away in the night after a few days.

All of the fifteen-year-olds in the village were now called up for military service, and the old men organized into the *Volkssturm*, or "home guard." They looked pathetic and ridiculous in their farmers' clothing, with gray armbands and old rifles. They dug anti-tank ditches halfway across the main street and piled sandbags behind them.

A perceptible difference in their attitude towards us now existed. Where before they had looked at us with hatred and contempt, they now regarded us with hatred and fear. They would usually shoot us a quick, venomous glance and then look at the ground and go away. We were no longer beaten by the farmers. Even our guards started to show a few traces of consideration.

An onlooker might think this dismay on the part of our masters would have been matched by a corresponding lifting of spirits on our side, but such was not the case. At the beginning of the war, no less a personage than Stalin had issued an order forbidding anyone to be taken to Germany for slave labor. We had all been ordered to kill ourselves rather than work for the enemy. We had quite obviously not done so. Repercussions were sure to follow. (As a matter of course, under Stalin's orders, every Soviet citizen who had done forced labor for the Germans was given a minimum sentence of 15 years upon their return to the USSR.) We were, therefore, as glum as our captors. It pleased us to realize that these assholes would get what they deserved, but our own base fate was uppermost in our minds.

Efrem, the squinty-eyed foreman who had first admitted me to the camp, seemed terrified and contrite.

"I didn't want to hit you, little brothers, the fucking Germans made me do it," he would say at every opportunity. We pretty much ignored him. We knew, and he knew, that upon the appearance of the first Soviet troops, he would be killed either by them or by one of us.

Soon, another 88 battery arrived in the village. Dirt-spattered guns were pulled by filthy prime movers—stubby, tracked vehicles with canvas sides into which equipment had been randomly tossed. We were called out to help unload the stuff. The guns were painted a yellowish-green and had yellow circles painted around the barrels. On the inside of the shields, small stenciled pictures showed the number of tank-kills each gun had scored. The highest number was 17, the lowest three and a half.

The gun crews handed equipment to us, which we piled in several heaps with the ammunition going in one stack, grenades in another, clothing in a third, and so on. The crews at first appeared to be old men. They were filthy and exhausted. Their faces were covered with stubble, dirt, and smoke. Their red eyes were fixed in a peculiar stare. In the American Army, that stare was known as the "thousand-mile stare." We had it, too. It is a look you get when the desolation and hopelessness inside you matches the desolation and hopelessness you see around you. There is only vacuum, only death. Nothing can be either hoped for or expected. Your life is an accident whose continued existence is somehow inexplicable and perhaps even slightly embarrassing.

I was standing in line behind the chess player when someone handed him two bundles of grenades. The German grenade was the size of a small tomato sauce can. Screwed into this was a wooden handle about a foot long. These bundles consisted of one whole grenade in the center and six heads wired to it in a circle with baling wire. This made a large super-grenade that might, in an emergency, blow a track off an enemy tank. I had seen pictures of this sort of thing in the newspaper but never had expected to see them in real life. I was impressed.

The chess player went off to deposit his burden, and I walked up to the side of the tractor.

"Careful with the *panzerfaust*," said a voice inside, and a *panzerfaust* was held out to me from under the canvas flap. It was painted a mustard yellow. Red lettering on the side of the launch tube said, "*Panzerfauspatrone*" and something else, and there were a couple of red painted arrows. I was completely terrified by the thing, but I took it automatically. It was surprisingly heavy. Taking a step back, I slipped in the mud and landed heavily on my ass.

A German soldier pulled me up. I expected to be beaten, kicked, or shot on the spot. His filthy old face looked at me, the dead eyes brushing across my dead eyes and continuing to the OST patch on my jacket. He took me to the other side of the tractor, handed me half a loaf of frozen, stale army bread, and directed me to a pile of equipment where he told me to separate greatcoats, packs, and belts into three separate piles. I hope he survived the war.

With the equipment unloaded and sorted, the Germans posted a guard and went into the surrounding houses to sleep. The piles of stuff were left in the snow. The guns stood in an untidy tangle with the barrels pointing every which way. The difference between this battery and the scrubbed, new Luftwaffe outfit that had preceded it could not have been more marked.

The next day, three Russian Mongols in German uniforms came into the camp. Large numbers of non-Germans fought on the German side. Some saw Hitler's attack on the Soviet Union as a crusade against Communism. This brought numerous Frenchmen, Norwegians, Flemings, and Finns into the SS. On the eastern side, various ethnic groups that had been overrun and ruled by the Russians and other Soviets saw the war as an opportunity for independence. This explained the Ukrainians, Balts, and Crimean

Tartars who were organized into special units. So many Cossacks joined the Germans that three full divisions of them operated on the Eastern Front and in Italy.

The Soviet general Vlassov, who had successfully defended Moscow against the Germans, was captured by the Germans when Stalin stupidly sacrificed Vlassov's division in the battle for Leningrad. Vlassov went over to the Germans and organized the R.O.A. (*Russkaya Osvoboditelnaya Armiya*), meaning "Russian Army of Liberation." This army consisted of several divisions and armored detachments of Russian ex-POWs. At the end of the war, they held Prague and tried to surrender to the Americans. The Americans turned them over to the Soviets, who drove tanks over them.

The Cossacks surrendered to the British, who turned them over to the Soviets. The Soviets shot them at a railhead in the British zone of occupation.

The people in these Armies of Liberation had mostly joined out of desperation. They had been Soviet soldiers and were being systematically starved by the Germans in various POW camps.

The eastern subhumans in German service were strictly forbidden to touch German women. So the three Mongols who appeared at our camp were looking for a woman. They had been sent to us by the local military commander. Our camp director gave them Elizabeth Motorcycle. She went off with them, giggling and sputtering, and was never seen by us again. Our chess player made a few witticisms about Tartars riding motorcycles, and then we forgot about her.

One Sunday, I suddenly remembered the German game warden who had been kind to me. It was our day off, so I went to see him. His cottage was empty, and the gamekeeper was absent.

While returning to camp in a depressed mood, a small soldier caught up to me. He carried a slung carbine and two dead rabbits. A blue and yellow patch on his sleeve read YBB (*Ukrainske Visvolne Viysko*), which stood for "Ukrainian Liberation Army." (Lots of imagination in the naming of these armies.)

"You are Ukrainian?" I said.

"I'm so fucked up I don't know what the fuck I am. Is that what you think you are? It doesn't matter a fuck. We will all be fucking dead soon," the small soldier said with incredible viciousness.

"You're losing the war, aren't you?" I asked.

"The fucking Germans are losing the fucking war. The filthy cocksuckers are running away and getting us all fucking killed. They start their counter-offensives and get a lot of people killed and then they run. You in a camp around here, kid?"

I said that I was.

"There any women in your camp I can fuck? I want to get fucked crosseyed before I get killed."

I said we used to have Elizabeth Motorcycle but that she had been given to the Tartars.

"Those slit-eyed, worthless motherfuckers. They fuck sheep, and then they eat them. They are lazy and diseased, all of them. Was your Elizabeth any good?"

I said no, she was ugly and smelled.

"Those Tartar motherfuckers won't know the difference. Are they killing you in your camp or just beating you?"

I said that we only got beaten up.

"Well, the Communists will be here in a week or two, and then they will kill you." The little soldier's tone was that of a mother telling an unruly child "all will be well soon."

The little man fascinated me. He exuded death, destruction, and viciousness. I had never met anyone before (or since) who was so upfront with qualities that one would expect in a mad-dog killer. I was not a little concerned about my safety, so when we parted on the outskirts of the village, seeing him leave didn't upset me much.

In the village square, the 88 battery was exercising its guns. The artillerymen elevated, depressed, and turned the heavy field pieces with rapidity. The villagers stood around gawking. The chubby local Nazi Party chief stood by the sandbags that lined the anti-tank ditch, loudly explaining to the baker's wife how the Soviet Army would be shattered and thrown back into the streets of Halbturn. He looked cheerful and confident. The baker's wife giggled and blushed.

In the camp, everything was gloom and depression. The chess player, of course, had a game going and huddled under his blanket, concentrating on his moves.

"Our people will be here in ten days," I said.

"What makes you think so?" asked the chess player.

"I met a Ukrainian soldier who told me," I explained.

"You Ukrainians are a backward and stupid people. Meaning no offense to you, personally," said the chess player. "The Bolsheviks will never get here."

Everyone laughed or smiled sadly.

"We are not stupid," I said. "My father is a professor, and he isn't like you. He isn't useless. He is a scientist."

"He's such an important person he couldn't even stop the Germans from throwing your ass in here with us," said the chess player. "Ukrainian professors don't know shit. That's why they need us Russians to run your silly little country," he continued, warming to his theme. "It's a good thing the Communists will kill you—otherwise you would have grown up to be a useless, stupid shit like your father."

A couple of the other men tried to calm him down, pointing out that I was only a kid.

"What the hell difference does that make?" said the chess player, suddenly bitter. "He will soon be dead along with the rest of us."

We went to sleep in a depressed mood with the inevitable Soviet plane rattling around above us.

In the morning, we were given a cup of artificial coffee and a piece of bread that, by now, would fall apart into some kind of dust at the slightest excuse, and were sent into the village to help the battery load and unload trucks. In the cold and in our condition, it was exhausting work.

At lunchtime, we received rations from the battery field kitchen. The cook gave us large, bronze-colored tins, one for every two people. Our joy was short lived when we opened these and discovered they contained green peas. Not only that, but the peas were frozen solid and covered with ice. Swallowing them was like eating ball bearings or lead shot. Holding them in your mouth until they thawed out produced an intense toothache. Pleased with his small victory for the fatherland, the cook surveyed us with a cynical smile.

Towards evening, the battery hitched up its guns and moved into the castle park where artillerymen started to set up emplacements. We were nearing spring now, and the snow was heavy and wet. We dragged ourselves back to camp through the wet snow with the frozen peas bouncing around inside us. Had the Soviets appeared at that moment and lined us up to be shot I don't think any of us would have given a fuck.

The next day, I found a British leaflet. It had a map showing the location of the fronts. I was astounded to discover that there was also a Western Front approaching Germany almost to the Rhine. When I mentioned this discovery to my fellows, they said, "Yes, but it is only a small front. The big front is here in the East."

A convoy of four trucks arrived with Czech laborers. They were young guys in good shape, and they were being supplied from home. They had plenty of bread. This came in the shape of large, round loaves, rather more civilian-looking than the brick-bread of the Germans.

The Czechs were generous and gave us their stale bread out of compassion or pity. We were the lowest human denominator. We had nothing to give, nothing to trade. We no longer even had ourselves.

The hours no longer crawled. The days began to rush by at an accelerating and frightening pace. The Czechs did short work of emplacing the 88's and departed, taking their wonderful bread with them.

"It won't be long now," they said. "Soon, you'll be free."

It seemed futile to explain to them that we would merely be going from one camp to another.

Then one day, as I was standing in line for my potato soup, clutching my enamel feeding bowl, I sensed a slight hint of vibration in the air. I looked around, but everyone else appeared merely intent on the forthcoming meal. I felt I must be wrong. But the feeling persisted.

By noon the next day, several others began to notice the vibration in the air. The day after that, individual concussions could be distinguished. Not a rolling waterfall of sound as it had been in Russia, but a quick series of shots followed by anywhere up to 30 minutes of silence and then another series of bangs. The concussions were now strong enough to rattle the window panes. We did not work that day.

The next morning, there was no breakfast. Towards midmorning a wood-burning civilian truck drove up, our guards clambered in, and the truck lurched away.

Suddenly, we were on our own. We went to the kitchen and found Efrem and the two slatterns who did the cooking also missing. We stood around in small groups, listening to the artillery fire, unsure of what to do next.

An army motorcycle with a sidecar went roaring past the camp. The noise of the engine jolted me into action. I walked briskly to the barracks, collected my food bowl and spoon, and took off, running down the road towards my family's camp. On the way to the castle, I had to pass two of the gun emplacements. The barrels were aimed, the full crews were in attendance, and the prime movers idled nearby with blue exhaust hanging in the air.

I ran up to the castle gates. Two Austrian farmers were finishing burying something. Wet, brown earth flew. I started through the gates.

"What do you want here?" asked one of them.

"My parents are here," I said.

"No one is here," said the farmer. "They all left yesterday evening except for those who didn't want to leave." He indicated the grave.

"Von Babow," I said.

"Ja! Du kennst den Von Babow?" he exclaimed, and they both laughed.

It seemed the morning before, Von Babow had called the lab together and ordered an evacuation. He said if anyone wanted to remain and wait for the Soviets, he would understand. Two families said they wanted to stay, and Von Babow had them executed.

Everyone else had been trucked to the nearby town of Bruck an der Leitha and put on a train for Ulm, in Bavaria. Von Babow had not gone with them.

The farmers were happily telling me their story, explaining the parts I had difficulty in understanding, when the 88s in the park started firing. There were four loud bangs followed by a bunch more in close succession. Then silence. We stood about for a moment, and then the farmers left. So did I. I headed for the railroad station where my friends and I had gone swimming so long ago.

I was walking down a very empty road when an army truck came tearing towards me. It skidded to a halt.

"Quick! Get in! The Russians are coming," someone yelled. "Mach schnell!"

I ran to the back of the truck and was dragged up.

"Die Russen sind schon hier," said a soldier, looking at my OST patch.

We raced through the park and out the other side where I had never been. The road was wide and empty. An overturned car with large holes in it lay in a ditch.

We drove through a deserted landscape. The occasional artillery shot was a reminder of life. Then we rounded a curve and saw a halftrack with a red-and-white-striped barrier. A military policeman with a shiny gorget hanging around his neck held up a red and white disc. We stopped. The driver and the other soldiers were questioned and directed to some point off the road.

I was told to keep moving. I did so until I came to another turn in the road and found some bushes. I sat among these, and, using my teeth and a very small twig, removed the OST patch from my jacket. Then I straightened my clothes, made certain my food bowl and spoon were secure, and set off towards the West.

7

The wonderful (or annoying) thing about roads is that one can never remain alone. Sooner or later, someone is certain to come along, and one's well-organized thoughts and plans are shredded by banal conversation and left behind with other roadside litter.

I did not walk for long before I was overtaken by a farm cart pulled by two horses. An old man with a mustache and a green felt hat drove, and two women and a child rode in the cart.

They stopped for me, and, after I had clambered on, started asking questions. Up until then, I had not realized the protection afforded me by my OST patch. No one cared about subhumans. Subhumans did not have parents or private lives or futures. Subhumans were not expected to live up to any standards of behavior or dress. I had not realized the safety, security, and freedom that went along with being a slave.

By removing my OST patch, I had transformed myself into an eleven-year-old human. Adults now felt justified in prying into my life. Where was I going? Where were my parents? What did my parents do? Why was I alone?

I replied that I had been separated from my family in an air raid. We had been on a train going to Ulm. Aircraft had attacked the train, and everyone had jumped off to seek cover. After the air raid, I had not been fast enough, and the train had started without me. Now I was trying to catch up or get to Ulm on my own.

It was an elegantly tight little story, all the more amazing for having been thought up as I went along. Living with my parents had made me into a proficient liar. The old man shook his head and uttered the customary "Jesus, Maria, and Joseph!" Then I was left alone.

I watched the dust rising from the other traffic on the road. There wasn't much. An occasional army truck or ambulance would pass us, and once a dispatch rider on a motorcycle went roaring past, headed back towards Halbturn.

There were still frequent sounds of artillery fire behind us, but nothing resembling a battle. The Germans were obviously falling back, and I thought I had better exchange my means of transport for something faster if I was going to get away from the advancing Red Army.

After a while, our road joined a two-lane paved highway. Here the traffic was crowded and frantic. The pavement was reserved for motorized traffic. Trucks, three abreast, moved away from the front. Horse-drawn carts used the shoulders of the road. As far as I could tell, nothing moved east. A lot of the horse carts, like the one I was in, held civilians. Other civilians rode in trucks. Everyone looked shabby, frightened, and depressed. It was obvious that the Germans were not merely defeated; they were routed.

The driver of my cart saw someone he knew pulled over a little distance off the road, so he, too, pulled over. He said he had to rest his horses. I stayed on the road and, by merely walking alongside it, got picked up by an army truck rigged out as a mobile bakery. They gave me a piece of bread, and I sat with my back against the cold oven and watched the retreat.

It went on mile after mile. At intervals, we would pass light anti-aircraft guns. These were sometimes mounted on halftracks, sometimes on full tank tracks. Most of them were the four-barreled variety. At times we passed burned-out vehicles and bomb craters, but none of these appeared to be especially recent. At some of the crossroads, military police stood with their shiny neck-gorgets and machine pistols. They would usually be standing around posts with direction pointers on them. The pointers bore a variety of Gothic symbols, letters, and numbers that must have meant something to those in the know. They did not mean much to me.

As it turned out, I was very lucky to have been picked up by the bakery truck. Their unit was on its way to defend Vienna, and so I had a ride all the way to the outskirts of that city.

Vienna was in the midst of preparation for the battle. Red, white, and black bunting hung on buildings, as did numerous German flags.

Slogans were painted on walls. *Wien bleibt deutsch!* (Vienna will remain German!) was the most frequent one. There were quite a few
destroyed buildings, but not nearly the devastation I would see later
in other cities.

There was something festive and feverish about the city. Bright
posters covered the advertising kiosks. I was especially taken with
one that showed a skeleton astride a two-engined bomber. The
skeleton was in the act of hurling a bomb at the only lighted window of an otherwise blacked-out city. There were also directions on
what to do in case of strafing attacks by aircraft. *Du kannst von einem
Tiefflieger nicht wegrennen* (You can't run away from a dive-bomber)
stated these signs. How true.

Vienna is dissected by numerous canals leading off the Danube
River. The bridges over many of these were being barricaded. There
were many SS troops around, looking smart and aggressive in their
spotted camouflage smocks. They were digging foxholes around the
edge of the Prater, and machine guns were being emplaced.

On the edge of a sidewalk in the middle of a bridge sat a dozen
or so old men. They had gray armbands with an eagle and the word
Volkssturm on them. Their old rifles leaned against the concrete railing. Some of the rifles had brass fittings. Their bolt handles stuck
straight out to the side. An old machine gun rested on its tripod.
It was a water-cooled gun that resembled the Russian Maxim, except that it was shorter, had a large funnel-shaped flash-hider, and
instead of the spade handles of the Maxim, the handles of this gun
were straight. Two ammunition boxes stood next to the gun.

The old men were eating pieces of black bread and chunks of
cheese. I stopped a safe distance from them and watched them eat.
They looked back at me. One of them asked me if I had a home.
I said I did not. They asked me where my parents were, and I said
I did not know. Finally, at long last, one of them asked me if I was
hungry and gave me a piece of bread.

When the old men got up to leave, I went with them. One of
the old men had trouble carrying the two boxes of machine gun
ammunition, and I offered to carry one. He let me. Carrying the
heavy box made me feel as though I belonged somewhere.

We walked for what seemed to be a long distance, the houses growing smaller and the old architecture giving way to cement workers' flats. Artillery shells fell off to our left, and something was being blown up. Pink smoke rose above the rooftops. Irises or daffodils or some damn vulva-shaped purple and white flowers were blooming in a front yard. It was April, and buds on the trees were breaking into leaf. Two Soviet fighter planes swept by overhead followed by the percussive rattle of their engines. I looked after them and saw sparks and smudgy smoke of an automatic anti-aircraft gun erupting far behind them. There was no sign of the Luftwaffe.

I felt very secure with this group of old men. They looked stable and sensible. Two of them kept switching off carrying the massive tripod. The tripod had toothed, crescent-shaped gear on its hind leg, which made it a bit awkward. The handle on the box of ammunition I was carrying dug into my hand, and I started carrying it in both hands in front of me. One of the old men took it from me, and the relief was instantaneous. I felt uplifted, a part of a great enterprise.

We passed two tanks of a type I had never seen before. There was no turret, just a low sloping carapace from the front of which an embarrassingly penis-shaped cannon projected like a steel erection. SS troopers sat about the tanks eating out of cans. One of them said something, and everybody laughed.

We came to the edge of the houses. There was a sloping field in front of us and more houses to our right front and some trees. Foxholes had been dug along the edge of the field, and an officer in a leather coat and a billed hat directed us to them. I stayed with the machine gun and the three old men that served it. They set up the gun, pointing it towards the houses across the field. One of the men opened an ammunition box and inserted a cloth cartridge belt into the right side of the gun. A few shells exploded near us. They arrived with a tearing noise and made a very loud bang. I saw one of them hit the roof behind us, but all it seemed to do was blow off a few roof tiles. Regular troops to our left and right wore camouflage smocks and steel helmets.

The foxhole was too deep for me. I had to put my elbows on the firing parapet and do a kind of pull-up to see over the dirt piled up in front. I was looking across at the houses in front of us when they began to disappear. There were bright flashes, lots of black smoke, and pieces of houses flying around. There were engine noises and lots of banging from somewhere behind us. The entire area to our front became a sea of boiling dust and smoke. Several machine guns fired in a rapid, hysterical manner, their streams of tracers disappearing into the dust.

The old man behind our machine gun moved the cocking handle three or four times and depressed both firing buttons. I was expecting a rapid burst of fire like the machine guns of the regular troops around us, but the old gun fired slowly, the individual shots clearly discernible. Instead of firing bursts, like the other machine guns, our old man grasped the two handles of the gun and pressed down on the triggers until the belt had run completely through the gun. His assistant on the right side fed in the second and last belt, and that was also fired through without pause. The gun began to steam, and the pile of empty cases underneath it grew.

When the second belt had been fired, the old men looked around and then clambered out of the trench. I took another look at our front. Something in all the dust and smoke was burning, adding still thicker black smoke to the cloud. I heard the distinctive ticking of a Soviet Maxim. There were several sharp, percussive noises that I at first took to be nearby rifle shots, but when I looked around, I did not see anyone firing. I followed the old men's example and took off.

Some mortars were emplaced two or so rows of houses from where we'd been earlier. They looked just like the one I had seen in our back yard in Kharkov four years previously. The crew was busily sliding shells into their muzzles, and the shells were popping out, climbing over the houses.

With my bunch of old men gone, I felt vulnerable and very much out of place. I retraced our journey at a much more rapid pace since I was no longer encumbered by a box of shells. When I passed the place where the tanks had been parked, I saw that they had left, which further increased my sense of unease and turned it almost into panic.

I passed a block of ruined houses. The walls of one of them had fallen out into the street, crushing a parked car. The car was completely flat, which for some reason struck me as very funny. I was half-running down the street of a city under shell-fire, giggling crazily to myself. From time to time, I would pass a group of soldiers, or a truck or ambulance would drive by. I saw no other civilians. Shells were falling all over the city, but I seemed to be traveling in some charmed circle since none of them came near me. It was the battle for Kharkov all over again. I felt as if time were running backward. Soon, I thought, it would be peace again, and I would be dunking the pigtails of arrogant little girls into inkwells. This thought made me laugh even harder.

It started to rain, a cold, driving rain that went right through to my skin and changed my mood from the ridiculous to the apprehensive and depressed.

I ducked into one of the bombed-out houses. It smelled of fire and old, decaying masonry. The upper floors had collapsed, and part of the ceiling of the lower floor hung down in a mass of lathes and plaster.

I stepped gingerly, afraid that the slightest noise would bring the entire mass of girders and bricks down on my head. A part of a staircase led up to a gray and rainy sky. Clothes lay scattered on the staircase.

My eyes fastened on a jacket of a strange pinkish color. I picked it up and discovered the color was mostly brick and plaster dust. Underneath it, the jacket was a dark gray. I tried it on, and it fit almost perfectly, if a bit large. Since it was considerably better than my own, I decided to keep it. It felt a little damp, but my shivering soon warmed it up. I also found a beige sweater with an Edelweiss design knitted into it, but it looked too Germanic, and I doubted I could explain how I had gotten it if anyone asked.

The rain died down to a drizzle, and I set out once again. In the middle of a wide street, a truck lay on its side, spilling a heap of wooden crates and blankets across the cobblestones next to it. A dead German soldier lay a slight distance away.

He was very young and very handsome. His overcoat was open and bunched up around his upper body. One arm was flung up behind his head. His long blond hair swept picturesquely along the cobblestones. Blood had crusted around his nose, but I could see no obvious wounds. Whenever I think about Vienna, I think of that empty street, the bursting of shells not too far away, and the dead German boy by his truck.

I was thinking about all the corpses I had seen in the war and why this corpse should have been of no more significance than the others when I heard a car behind me. I moved over to the side of the roadway, but the car slowed, and the driver sounded his horn.

I turned, surprised to see a civilian car with two old men in it. The car was a dark blue Adler, and the men wore suits and overcoats. One of the men reached and opened the back door and motioned for me to get in.

I was simultaneously relieved to have a ride, overwhelmed by being allowed to ride in the back of a passenger car, and apprehensive about what the grown-ups might do when they discovered I was not one of them. But all went well. I explained in my broken German that I was trying to find my family in Ulm. The old men nodded perfunctorily and went back to their conversation. Off we went.

We drove past ruined and burned houses. We stopped at checkpoints where one of the old men showed the military police some papers that got us promptly waved through. I wish I had understood more German, for surely these old men must have been important people, and I would have been interested in what they were saying to one another. But I was much like a lost and frightened puppy picked up by kind strangers. I cowered in the back of the car as it took me out of Vienna, away from the front, and finally deposited me at a railway station in a small village called Gerolding.

Gerolding was a truly picturesque village nestled between strikingly green mountains. A small white church perched atop a steep hill. A stone wall surrounded the church and its adjacent graveyard.

By climbing the wall and standing on top of it, one could see the Danube. Twin-tailed, twin-engined American fighter planes of the type the Germans called "Tiefflieger" were strafing some barges in the river. Two of the planes took turns making runs on the barges. The plane would dive, pull out just above the water, and head for the barges. White streaks appeared on the river in front of the plane and reached for the barge. Then the plane would pull up, and the other one would take its place. After a few minutes one of the barges drifted onto the bank and the planes flew away. I walked back to the station.

A large crowd milled about, waiting for the train, which was in the process of being assembled. When it pulled up, it consisted of freight and passenger coaches pulled by an old locomotive. We swarmed over the train, and soon it was overcrowded. I wound up in a freight car with a swarm of soldiers, nursing mothers, and other assorted riff-raff of various nationalities. We squabbled for corners and other mini-territories. Family groups and other social assemblies established themselves amidst their packs and bundles and tried to ignore each other as much as possible. Infants screamed, soldiers laughed and smoked, foreign refugees spoke in near whispers.

The train jerked, stopped, and started again. We moved slowly past some bombed-out sidings and gathered speed. Wound in a cocoon of steam, smoke, and cinders, we rattled through scenic countryside.

Suddenly, we stopped. Railway personnel crunched through the gravel alongside the train screaming, "*Alles raus!*"

The herd that had grown quiet now came back to life. We clambered out. Packs and equipment belts were passed down. Babies were slung under pendulous breasts, and suitcases were hefted. We set off at a laborious pace, trudging past the stopped train.

Emerging from behind the train, we passed into reality again. The entire railbed was torn up. Huge yellow bomb craters covered the fields on either side. They were so fresh, water had not yet begun to accumulate in them. Large, gray bomb splinters lay in the bottoms of the craters. The rails had been twisted and flung far off the rail embankment and into the fields.

Wreckage lay along the bottom of the embankment, and it was not until I saw the locomotive that I realized I was looking at the remnants of another train. Only a few sections of roofs were recognizable and of course the wheels. The carriages themselves had been separated into broken planks and bits of sheet iron that were blown about like street litter in a strong wind.

A few bits and pieces remained near our path. Among them was an upside-down army helmet. Its brand-new tan leather liner was smeared and clotted with a brownish-black jam-like substance around which bluebottle flies buzzed in a leisurely manner.

We trudged along under an unseasonably warm April sun. Soon the soldiers and the younger, single men had outdistanced the old and the family groups encumbered with small children and numerous bundles. I became painfully aware of the superiority of the backpack over all forms of luggage. The suitcase appeared especially unsuitable for long portages.

Before long, discarded possessions piled up along the sides of our passage. First to go were rope-tied cardboard boxes. These were followed in short order by square, sharp-cornered suitcases. Word filtered down the column that another train waited two kilometers down the track. While most of us took heart from this announcement, a few of the older and the more loaded down stopped or sat on their bundles with expressions of bleak despair on their faces.

One of those was a kindly looking, pleasant-faced woman burdened with a backpack, a suitcase, and a shopping net. The handles of the net, being rather thin, cut into her hand. She stood by the side of the line flexing her hand and looking bewildered and sad.

Even at the age of eleven, I was a sucker for sad-faced, bewildered women, so I offered to carry her shopping net, seeing how my only possession was my feeding bowl stuffed inside my shirt. She looked around and asked where my parents were. I found the question rather deflating to my newfound ego. I proceeded to explain in my broken German how my parents had gone on to Ulm and how I just finished carrying machine gun ammunition for the Volkssturm in Vienna.

To my surprise, the lady looked neither approving nor reassured nor even particularly interested. Instead, her sad expression deepened, and she looked at me with pity and horror. We started to walk again, her shopping net swinging about my knees and cutting into the palms of my hands as it had into hers. When we had to clamber down one side and up the other of a large bomb crater, she put out her free hand to help me up. I asked her if she was German and she said yes, of course, she was. I then asked her if she did not believe in final victory, and she looked at me sadly, put out her hand, and pushed me forward.

We were passing a small group of houses, and a woman and two small girls came down from one of them with buckets of water. The little girls offered us cups of water and curtsied as we accepted them. That was the first time in my life I had seen a girl curtsy, let alone to me. It made me feel very strange. The war was certainly expanding my social horizons.

And then miraculously we were past the bombed-out section, and there, as promised, was another train. Much as the last one, it had a mixture of passenger coaches and cattle cars. Most people were heading for the passenger coaches. Mindful of my status, I clambered up into a cattle car, and, to my surprise, the German lady followed.

We were able to get a corner and, placing her pack and suitcase in front of us, secured enough space to stretch our legs. People kept arriving, and the car was filling up. An old lady with two kids was the last to climb in. The three of them collapsed on the floor, staring at the rest of us with dull eyes.

With the usual jerky motion, the train started. We experienced no laborious shunting from one track to another this time. We took off and kept going. At first, everyone was tired and relieved to be on the train. For a while, almost no one spoke, and the sound of the wheels put everyone in a soporific mood. Many slept.

I awoke what must have been a short time later. People were beginning to stir. A soldier, one of a group of four, pulled a mouth organ out of his pocket, knocked it on the palm of his left hand,

and started playing some semi-sad, semi-jaunty German tune. The German lady next to me woke up. She stretched, smiled at me, and started to ask questions. I told her I had been living with my parents at a scientific institution and had become separated from them when they were moved to Ulm. I did not mention the camp.

The lady told me her name, which I promptly forgot, not being good with names, and we solemnly shook hands. She then started to tell me about herself. Since my German was not very good at the time, and since she spoke rapidly, I only got the general gist of it. She had been working in some office or agency. Her husband had been missing in Russia for a couple of years, or else he was dead. She was going to some unpronounceable town in Bavaria to stay with an aunt. She kept ending her sentences with questions, or at least in a questioning tone of voice. She also kept reaching out and touching my shoulder.

For the past four years, her people and her government had gone to considerable lengths to convince me of my personal, and my people's general, inferiority. I had seen my fellows cheat, steal, lie, and inform on one another, and they had even devoured their dead. I was convinced of and had learned to live with this assessment of myself. I knew I was the absolute racial bottom of the human species. In this knowledge, there was security and peace. Now, this silly woman treated me as someone I clearly was not. I resented this and it confused me. I resented her and was suspicious of her. I kept expecting her to sense this. Didn't the stupid woman know anything? Yet she didn't catch on, just kept talking, ending her sentences with those ridiculous questioning words, reaching out and touching me in that irritating fashion. Finally, and I was not certain of this due to my imperfect knowledge of the language, I think she actually asked me to go to her aunt's with her. One final interrogative sentence, one final touch on my shoulder, and she looked at me expectantly.

I put words together in my mind, checked them for accuracy, and used what I thought to be a good German sentence. "Leider bin ich Untermensch," I said. Which expressed the idea that while it was nothing personal, I was unfortunately subhuman, and we really did not belong in the same circles.

Something happened to the woman's face. She looked around quickly and started talking in an intense semi-whisper. Again, much of what she said was beyond my comprehension, but I got the idea that she did not agree with the racial theories of the government and, in any event, what did it have to do with us personally?

I was saved from answering by an argument that broke out between two soldiers. One was a Hungarian SS trooper. The other was an Asiatic Russian Cossack. The Hungarian had been sitting with two young women, cutting a long piece of salt-pork into little squares with his pocket knife and feeding them to the two girls.

I am not certain what the cause of this argument was, but the two of them jumped up and, balancing themselves against the rocking of the carriage, started yelling at one another. The Hungarian yelled in German, the Cossack yelled in Russian. I think they didn't come to blows because the train was moving and their footing was very uncertain. They sat down again, and the argument sputtered out. People who had been watching the two soldiers with alarm or anticipation went back to their conversations.

I asked the Cossack where his unit was, and he said somewhere around Prague. He was surprised that I was Russian. Since I wore a German-style jacket and sat with a German lady, he had assumed I was German.

The German lady still acted as if she expected an answer from me. She made me feel uncomfortable. I have often wondered since the war whether she was a genuinely concerned and kind person, or whether she was a frustrated and depressed middle-aged woman who wanted to suck a young boy's dick.

It is so difficult to think well of others. A person feels such a fool upon finding out he has been taken advantage of yet once again.

Towards evening, the train pulled into a sizeable town. The station had suffered a recent air raid and was the most devastated place I had seen in Germany up to that time. There were craters inside craters, burned-out skeletons of freight cars, carriages standing on end. A flatcar tilted precariously. It still carried the new model Panther tank with its exceptionally long cannon pointing into a bomb crater.

We stared at all this devastation silently as the train slowly pulled into the passenger part of the rail terminal. A glass dome had once covered it, but all of the glass had been blown out with the remaining iron latticework stark and desolate against the darkening sky.

Here we were told we would have to change trains. We stumbled out onto the platform, and almost immediately, the air raid sirens sounded. I felt more or less stuck with the German lady and was regretting the impulse that had led me to help her.

We walked out of the station building together. Searchlights swept the sky to the west of us. The dark town smelled of fire and rotting damp things. Phosphorescent arrows had been painted on walls of buildings with the word *Luftschutzraum* stenciled on them. They indicated the direction of air raid shelters. I helped the German lady into a large cellar with wooden benches along the walls. Firefighting equipment hung on pillars supporting the ceiling. I saw to it that she settled down comfortably and then excused myself and went back up the stairs. The man at the door did not want to let me out, but I told him I was looking for a younger brother and made my escape.

It felt rather wonderful to be free again. It was cold and drizzling, but the searchlights were beautiful. I sat on a recessed stairway under the overhang of a large, ruined house and watched. Many aircraft engines sounded overhead. Anti-aircraft guns fired from some distance away, and the shell explosions sparkled in the dark sky. A plane dropped brilliant red, green, and white flares. Bombs began to drop. All this was far enough away for me to feel safe. Occasionally, an anti-aircraft shell splinter landed on the cobblestones, but nothing else came near me.

After a while, the planes went away, the guns stopped, and most of the searchlights went out, although a couple continued to sweep the sky in wide, aimless arcs. I went back to the railway station.

A train was loading for Munich, and I got into a compartment with six soldiers and an elderly civilian. I felt great. The raid was over, I had given the slip to the German woman, and I was on another train.

We hadn't been traveling for more than fifteen minutes when the elderly civilian began to talk. He started by asking the soldiers a few questions. The soldiers, who had been quietly conversing among themselves, answered civilly but with obvious reluctance. They apparently wanted nothing to do with the intense old man who now unleashed a veritable torrent of words on them. When they tried to argue or say anything, he simply raised his voice. As far as I could tell, the old man had been a lieutenant in the First World War and had finished the war as a company commander. He went on and on about the virtues of the German soldier. Courage, loyalty, discipline, and initiative in combat situations were mentioned so often that they became a background mantra to what the man had to say.

His message was that the war would have been won long ago if it had been left to the soldiers and their brilliant Führer, who had also been a simple soldier in the Great War. The problem lay with the officer corps, especially the senior officers who were lazy, incompetent, corrupt, and treasonous. The generals were the ones betraying the Führer, the soldiers, and the German Nation. The old man droned on and on, his voice grew hoarse, and spittle appeared at the corners of his mouth. The soldiers were uneasy.

I had never heard of the officers' plot and the bungled assassination of Hitler the previous year and so was astounded. What surprised me was not the content of the old man's talk, which I took to be drivel, but rather the fact that no one arrested him. I kept expecting one of the soldiers to haul his rifle from the overhead baggage rack or to run the old guy through with a bayonet or even to bust him in the mouth, but none of those things happened. The old man sputtered out and went to sleep, and the soldiers resumed their conversation.

I must have fallen asleep as well because suddenly it was daylight, the train had stopped, and people were rushing off the train to the shouts of "*Alles Raus!*" (Alarm!)

I tumbled out of the train. It had stopped in a wide green field with the engine hidden in a cut through the crest of a small hill. The cut was too short for the whole train. It protected only the locomotive, the coal-tender, and one-and-a-half coaches. The rest of the coaches were left standing in the field. People were running towards a forest about one hundred meters away. On the other side of the train lay a wide field, and on the other side of the field stood a complex of large, red brick buildings.

A group of four-engined bombers flying towards the buildings had caused the excitement. I counted sixteen bombers, and they flew much lower than I had ever seen them before. The bombers looked sinister and dark against the gray sky. There was no anti-air-craft fire. We had a single-barreled 37 mm cannon on our train. It had been swiveled towards the bombers and was following them, but it never fired. Possibly the planes were too high.

While they were still some distance away from us, two smoke trails broke away from one of the lead planes. Dense and very black, they arched over the train, reaching out like terrifying tentacles, and landed just the other side of the large buildings. Sticks of bombs now began to fall away from each plane. They followed the path of the smoke trails. When they landed, huge, black explosions obscured the buildings. There was no flame, only black tendrils of dirt and smoke rising and flying in all directions.

By now, I was down on the ground with everyone else, feeling the blast waves rolling over me. The sound of the explosions reached us several seconds after the bombs began to explode. The sound was surprisingly dull, not at all like the sharp explosions of the Soviet artillery shells in Vienna.

When the explosions stopped, the buildings were still there, but their outline had changed somehow. I couldn't quite make out what the change was because the locomotive let out three blasts and everyone started running back towards the train.

Either I had been more frightened than the others, or else, being unencumbered by baggage, I had run faster and farther away from the train. In any event, I now found myself almost the last person to reach the train. It started to move, and I jumped on the hind steps of the next-to-the-last carriage. It was a passenger carriage of the type with many enclosed compartments along the left side and a long walkway along the right side. Somewhat preoccupied and confused by the bombing raid and the run for the train, I barged into the first compartment and found myself face to face with a group of plump girls in gray Luftwaffe uniforms.

Both they and I were startled by my sudden, breathless appearance. They giggled. I stared. One girl who was uglier and bigger than the others had wedged into the corner of the bench. Her skirt had ridden up, exposing fat, pink thighs with an interesting dark gap in the middle. I stared at this partly from interest, partly because I couldn't think of anything else to do. The girl said something to her friends and opened her legs more. She was wearing a pair of gray-knitted boxer shorts. I blushed to the tops of my ears, and the girls burst out laughing. I ran out of their compartment pursued by the laughter and rapidly walked to the other end of the corridor, which was blocked by a large family of Balkan or Slavic refugees. I couldn't make out their language at all and they, for their part, tried to ignore my presence.

The journey continued in this uncomfortable fashion for a day or so until we came to a sizeable station where everyone was again requested to transfer to another train. Given the fantastic intensity of air attacks, it is remarkable that the trains ran with any regularity at all. Several times each day we would pass wrecked trains and long lines of workers repairing the tracks. At that time, I considered them merely a nuisance because their work also forced the train to slow down.

I wish I could remember all the names of all the places where the more significant events occurred, but many of them have slipped away. In any case, as the herd of us got off the train and mixed with the other herds from other trains, the air raid warning went off. We were ordered to go to our air raid cellars. I delayed as much as I could. The station had a number of rail-mounted four-barreled anti-aircraft guns parked on different sidings, and as I walked by the tail end of one of the herds, I noticed an unusual amount of activity among their crews. Thanks to my delaying tactics, the air raid shelter was filled by the time I reached it, so I was again able to seek shelter in a doorway and watch.

The first sign of the air raid was a single German fighter plane, an ME-109, that came screaming low over the rooftops and disappeared to the east. In about ten minutes, it was followed by the high-pitched noise of many engines, quite different from the heavy droning of the four-engined bombers to which by now I had become accustomed. A large gaggle of aircraft approached rapidly. They were the twin-engined, twin-fuselage type that the Germans usually called *Tiefflieger* and the Americans, P38 Lightnings. The planes were painted green and had red spinners.

Every anti-aircraft gun in the station now opened up. It was fantastic. Quadruple trails of smoke-trailing tracer shells rose high into a blue sky where, at the end of their flight, they exploded into large yellowish-brown clouds. Flaming P38s cartwheeled all over the sky, trailing fire and black smoke. They hit the ground and skidded along, shedding parts of themselves and dripping fire. They had flown far too low for any of their pilots to bail out.

I think I counted six planes shot down in what appeared to be seconds. Then it was all over. The all-clear sounded. People scrambled out of the air raid shelters and headed for the station. The entire raid was over in minutes. I couldn't get over how fast it had been. The clouds from exploding anti-aircraft shells still hung in the sky, and the wreckage of downed planes still burned and smoked on the ground, and here I was climbing onto yet another train.

As we were pulling out of the station, we passed one of the downed P38s. One of its twin fuselages had shorn off, but the front part remained intact. The pilot's canopy was closed, and smoke had blackened the red spinners. It was a striking change from the terrifying and deadly force that had menaced us only minutes before. I felt sorry for it, not for the man who had flown it, but for the machine itself. Without its power and purpose, it was as pathetic as a human corpse.

Two army gendarmes and two civilian policemen forced their way through the carriages, checking documents. As in previous such checks, they ignored me because of my age. Almost everyone submitted to these checks with good humor, the exceptions being various eastern refugees who were frightened of anything having to do with papers and uniforms. This time everyone was in a good mood thanks to the air raid. It felt wonderful to be alive and to see that which had tried to kill you defeated.

After an uneventful afternoon and night, we pulled into a town called Freising where we were supposed to change trains for Munich. I walked outside the station and heard my name called. I turned to see a family that had been in my parents' camp at Halbturn. They said that my family had only left Freising that morning, bound for Munich and Ulm. They gave me some bread and directed me to a nearby refugee center where, they said, I might get fed and inquire further about my family.

I found the meeting itself shocking and the conversation distasteful. I had come to view myself as a free adult, and being talked down to upset me. I wanted to run, to escape, but instead found myself trudging down the highway to the refugee center. I picked up a stick and decapitated roadside thistles. I was hungry and felt humiliated. To make matters worse, when I got there, the place turned out to be some sort of information center that had no information of any use to me. It was a typical grown-up fuckup.

I was contemplating returning to the railroad station and waiting around for the train to Munich that was supposed to leave at 1:30 p.m. when the air raid alarm went off. I stood in the courtyard of the information center with a group of ten or eleven other Russians and watched events unfold. This was a raid by four-engined bombers. Freising must not have been important enough for permanent anti-aircraft emplacements because I do not remember any anti-aircraft fire.

That morning stands out in crystalline clarity. It was about 10:30, and the sun reflected off the silver bombers as they approached in precise formation. Three planes dropped the by now familiar smoke markers. When I saw them before under cloudy conditions, the smoke had appeared sooty-black. Now in bright sunshine, it looked dark brown and somehow curly, like the hair on a large dog or teddy bear. The smoke markers curved and fell somewhere around the railroad station.

At this point, the other planes began to drop bombs, and I, along with the other sightseers, stampeded into a small concrete cellar. It is amazing how long it takes for a bomb to fall. I saw them separating from the planes while I was still standing in the courtyard. By the time I got into the cellar, I could hear them falling. Where German bombs had made a screaming sound, the American variety simply sounded like artillery shells, producing a noise like the tearing of cloth. The American bombing raids were so massive that added psychological effects, like a screaming siren, would not, could not, have contributed to the terror.

The train station was at least a kilometer away from us, yet when the bombs started landing, the windows high up on the wall of our cellar blew in. The blasts picked us up off the cement floor and threw us down again. This went on and on, one perilously stretched-out minute after the next.

There was an old woman in the cellar with us, and she would get up on her knees for the few moments before the blasts tossed her down again and start crossing herself while mumbling prayers. I had been raised in a thoroughly anti-religious society and indeed believed that religion was "opium for the masses." But now, with death imminent, and with absolutely nothing else that could be done, I began emulating the old woman.

"Hey, kid," said one of the Russian men, "Cut that shit out. You are acting like a cocksucker. Men don't act this way. Besides, I'm scared, too, and if you don't quit, I might start doing it, too. If you are going to die, die like a man."

I stopped. Many years later, I remembered the man's admonition and felt ashamed of myself. I remember it still and hope he survived the war and is somehow all right. Of all the things said to me by adults, that one made the most sense.

The bombing seemed to last an eternity though it must only have lasted some fifteen to twenty minutes. Every time I thought it was finally over, a new wave of explosions would toss us about the cellar, and my relief at still being alive would evaporate. Then suddenly it was over.

We came out of the cellar into a different world. The first thing that struck the eye was that the sunlight had changed. Where before everything had been sharp and sparkling, now things were fuzzy and diffused as if immersed in a fog. We were inside a gigantic cloud of dust. Broken glass covered the ground like ice crystals.

Emergency vehicles and military trucks started going by outside, headed towards the station. I followed them. After walking for some five hundred meters, I passed the first corpse. A plump woman lay in a ditch, a bicycle on top of her.

On the other side of the ditch, a field with long rows of cabbages extended towards a group of greenhouses. The rows were now interrupted by a couple of bomb craters, and the greenhouses did not appear to have a single pane of glass left.

The station buildings, as well as other buildings around them, were either obliterated or burning. Rails were bent, twisted, and scattered. Railway carriages were tossed about like matchboxes. A stench of fire, explosives, and shit hung in the air.

There had been a troop train and a couple of civilian trains in the station at the time of the raid. Many of the people had been either crowding the station buildings or lying about on a wide, grassy slope by the side of the tracks.

These people were now rearranged geometrically and anatomically in diverse kaleidoscopic patterns. There were circular and semicircular swatches of them and their possessions around the bomb craters that now disfigured the meadow. Some of them were very white, others yellow or gray. Some had burst or had pieces missing. Others were unrecognizable bits. Gobbets of flesh stuck to hard surfaces. Blue, dark red, yellow, and greenish entrails and organs hung from downed and dangling power lines.

The smell of flesh, feces, explosives, and smoke was indescribable. It was a living thing that clawed its way into your lungs, your heart, and your mind. Had it not been for the dirt thrown up by the bombs, the multicolored clothing of the dead women and children would have made them look like bizarre flowers scattered in a complex pattern across the field. The gray-green soldiers blended into the background except for where the brick-red, lurid splashes of arterial blood commanded attention.

For some reason, I had always considered death as something sinister, somber, and dark. In this place, it ruled with bold effrontery: the multicolored, festively scattered innards, the bright clothes, and the cheerfully crackling flames combined with the horrible stench and the sunny spring day to create the atmosphere of a picaresque and incomprehensible carnival.

I wandered around in a state of shock. I picked up an army ration can lying by a burst-open ration satchel that had been torn from a soldier's belt, and stuffed it inside my shirt. (When I opened it later, it contained a rich yellow cheese that made me ill and gave me cramps.) I also picked up a felt-covered army canteen.

After some time, a stormtrooper in a brown uniform with a swastika armband put his hand on my shoulder and asked me where my parents were. I said I did not know. He led me across the road from the station to where a group of badly shocked people sat around, waiting for someone to do something about them. Some of them shook, some cried, others just stared straight ahead. A few of the Red Cross ladies were concentrating their attention on a girl who screamed and thrashed about. The trooper told me to sit down and then left. I waited until he disappeared and then snuck away.

I could not stand to be near these people who had in some horrible way been broken. I could no longer tolerate the smell or the proximity of the war or all the scattered corpses, alive only a short time ago, many of whom must have arrived on the same train as I had. I felt that in another minute I must burst, contributing my own viscera to those so bountifully strewn about the Freising Bahnhof. I followed the tracks, heading west.

After walking for a while, I sat down on a rail tie and looked around. In the distance hung the smoke cloud from the bombed station, but around me, the sun shone, and flowers bloomed. The air smelled clean except for the not-unpleasant tar and creosote scent of the rail ties. Everything was familiar, orderly, and safe.

I unstrapped the little plastic cup from the top of my new canteen and unscrewed the aluminum top. To my surprise, the canteen contained not water but a sour white wine. After spitting out the first mouthful, I was going to throw the rest of it away when it occurred to me that it had been purchased by a man now dead. I forced myself to drink a few mouthfuls and then poured the rest out.

I went down to investigate a small creek or large puddle below the railway embankment. It turned out to be full of tadpoles and frogs. I started playing war with the frogs, throwing rocks at them. Then the wine went to my head. I filled up the canteen from the puddle and sat there drinking from it and giggling to myself.

It suddenly occurred to me that I was no longer puzzled by the war. I understood the war completely, and it was all right. The war was a war of adults against children. The adults had all the planes, all the bombs, and all the guns, but the children were going to win. We would win because the adults had to fuck and that would create more children and more children still, and now that I knew what the war was all about, I could explain it to the others. Sooner or later, we would have a children's revolution. We would kill our parents and everyone else who had hair on their genitals.

I sat at the edge of the puddle and planned my revolution while a work train went by headed for the bombed station. After a while, I heard voices and looked up. It was evening now, and a line of people with bags and suitcases walked along the tracks. I joined them and was told a train waited to take us to Munich. We only had to walk two kilometers to reach it. I stumbled along with everyone else. My head began to hurt.

8

This last train ride seemed quite different from any other I had ever undertaken or was ever to take again. While the carriage wheels set up the usual hypnotic knocking across rail junctions, I went off into a near-narcotic state. Every time I looked at a wall or a ceiling in the compartment, I thought I saw bits of flesh adhering to it. Whenever I looked at any of my traveling companions, I saw them as corpses.

Fortunately, it soon got dark, the train slowed greatly, and I shivered and whimpered undisturbed until morning. We stopped at some forlorn siding for a while. There was a full moon, and we were next to a long line of flatcars loaded with shot-down bombers. It was easy to tell the British planes from the American ones. The British bombers had been painted black, they had long pointed engines, and their machine gun turrets bore four skinny, inconsequential-looking barrels. The American planes were silver, the engines were round and stubby, and the machine gun turrets carried two massive, heavy-caliber guns.

In the morning, we started passing large numbers of anti-aircraft guns mounted on flatcars and left standing on sidings. Although their barrels were decorated with numerous rings denoting shot-down aircraft, the guns appeared to be unmanned.

Shortly afterward, the train went into a long curve and slowed down. Many FW-190 fighter planes sat in a field alongside the tracks. They had yellow spinners and wingtips, camouflage paint on top, light blue on the bottom. Most of them burned brightly and were falling to pieces. Some Luftwaffe soldiers stood nearby and watched. Everyone on the train who could get to a window also watched. No one said anything. The usual murmur of conversation stopped.

We arrived in Munich towards noon on a sunny spring day. Before the train came to a complete halt, a couple of soup carts appeared. It seemed that the local Nazi Party was attempting to lift the morale of the hordes of refugees from the eastern parts of the Reich by feeding them soup. Everyone on the train started looking around for containers. I produced my camp feeding bowl and promptly got it filled with highly spiced vegetable soup. It was the first hot food I had had in days, and it was delicious.

Word came that train tracks all around the city were bombed and no trains would be leaving until evening. I set out to see the city. There was nothing to see, but that nothing felt ominous.

The whole of Munich was one great ruin. Partial houses stared out on the street from empty windows. In places, entire streets had been completely obliterated, having become only continuous brownish-red fields of shattered brick with here and there a chimney standing up or a pipe sticking out of the rubble. In places, the cloying stench of decomposing bodies made me speed up while trying not to breathe.

American airplanes circled continuously overhead, so air raid alarms only sounded when an actual bombing was either in progress or about to occur. Here I saw a new type of American plane for the first time. The plane had a very streamlined body, two engines, and wings that slanted back from the engines.

A couple of Hitler Youths standing in a doorway with an aircraft recognition booklet told me that the planes were called C47 Dakota, that they were transport planes, and that the Americans were using them for long-range reconnaissance, proving they were running out of resources and were about to lose the war.

A truck came rattling by with a single-barreled 20 millimeter anti-aircraft cannon mounted in the back. A German stood behind the cannon wearing a Luftwaffe uniform. His jacket was unbuttoned. He wore officer's boots. The expression on his face was tragic.

I went back to the railroad station to wait for a train. There were two gangs of prisoners clearing rubble around the station. One gang consisted of Belgian prisoners of war. They wore uniforms that had once been blue or had been dyed blue. The blue had now turned to violet, lending them an operatic air.

Guarded by the SS, the other gang wore strange striped uniforms. No one went near them. I was told in a hushed tone that they were concentration camp inmates and that it was better not to go near "people like that."

The Belgians were lackadaisical about their "work." They mostly sat on heaps of bricks knocking the old mortar off the bricks, and then throwing them over their shoulders. The concentration camp inmates did whatever they were doing with a fearful intensity.

In the afternoon, there was a minor bombing raid. At least, it appeared minor in comparison with the one in Freising. I went down into a very large air raid shelter under the station. By this time in the war, rumor had it that if you were buried under rubble in an air raid shelter, no one was going to bother digging you out. According to folk wisdom, the people in the air raid shelters were the ones you could smell while walking through the ruins.

Possibly for that reason, the air raid shelter I found myself in was not all that crowded. I sat with my back to the wall and listened to the bombs explode. Most of the explosions seemed some distance away.

A flurry of excitement arose near the door, and two of the concentration camp inmates brought in a third who had been wounded. Their guard made them leave the man lying on the floor and then chased them back out into the air raid. The injured man lay on the floor and moaned. His skin was brown, like old furniture, and his head had been shaved to stubble. He had a red triangle sewn to his striped jacket.

His yellowish eyes roamed about the cellar and came to rest on a young Catholic priest sitting against a wall some distance away. The wounded man said something to a woman sitting near him, and she walked over and said something to the priest. The priest waved his arms and spoke volubly to the woman. She came back and spoke to the wounded man and the people around him. What she said started a buzz of conversation. Several people looked at the priest, who got up and moved to a farther wall. It seemed that the inmate had asked for Last Rites, and the priest had replied that he was a German priest and did not give Last Rites to enemies of the Reich.

The wounded man continued to lie on the floor and moan. Someone covered him with a blanket. When the air raid ended, the two inmates and the guard who had brought him down took him away again. The priest left the shelter and disappeared into the crowd.

In the evening, a train came. It was on the way to Kempten, which was in the same general direction as Ulm. I boarded with a large crowd. We were shunted around for a long time and moved very slowly over insecurely laid tracks. Finally, the train sped up for the long haul, and almost everyone went to sleep.

A group of soldiers sat in the two seats behind mine. They differed from all the other soldiers in the carriage in that they were not armed. Neither did they have any cartridge belts or equipment. There were six of them, and four of the six wore Iron Cross ribbons in their buttonholes.

These soldiers were quietly and happily drunk. Whenever I got thirsty and took a swig from my canteen, one of them would say *Schnapps mein Reisekamerad*, and all the rest of them would laugh. This annoyed nearby passengers who were trying to sleep. Finally, some woman told them to shut up, and the soldier who had been doing all the talking quietly and in a genteel manner called her an old cunt. The woman said something to her husband. The husband, quite prudently, in my opinion, refused to become involved, saying that the soldiers were drunk and irresponsible.

The woman started bitching at her husband, and other passengers, including the soldiers who had started the whole thing, yelled at the woman to shut up so they could go to sleep. Every time the woman began to wind down, the soldier behind me would quietly say, "You old cunt." This was said just loud enough for the woman to overhear, and she would start up again. Finally, she burst into tears and went into the bathroom. The carriage quieted down.

Just after sunrise, we pulled into a town called Memmingen, and everyone was told to leave the train. No trains were going any farther west. I asked the soldier who had been giving everyone a hard time the night before when railway service would resume, and he said, "After the final victory." His friends giggled. I asked when the final victory would be, and that really sent them into convulsions. They patted me on the shoulder and left.

Memmingen station had been bombed quite recently and, except for an absence of corpses, looked very similar to the station at Freising. There were the same bomb craters, the same twisted rails, the same disintegrated and up-ended rail carriages. The buildings near the station had also been hit, and many of the ruins still smoldered. Tired-looking firemen and SA troopers pushed burning bits of rubble about the cobblestones or stood leaning on shovels.

Fortunately, the bombed-out section soon ended, and I walked out into an undamaged German town. Memmingen was a medieval town. It had narrow cobblestoned streets and brightly painted houses with steep tiled roofs. One major highway ran through town. The highway entered and left the town through covered gates in the old city wall. One of the gates still had a guard tower over it, and embedded in the tower wall was a rusting cannonball that had been fired into it in the seventeenth century.

At the time, I was not at all interested in the town's history. As long as there had been a functioning railroad, I had had a purpose. Although I paid lip service to looking for my family, I realized I didn't give a damn. It bothered me, however, that I now had no plan of action. I found myself in a dynamic limbo, a perplexing situation in which there was nothing to do but wait.

Preoccupied with these thoughts and feelings, I wandered around town until I came to a *gasthaus* (small inn) called The Black Swan. There seemed a great deal of activity of some civilian sort going on. People kept going in and out with obvious purpose. The highway ran past the establishment, and there was considerable military traffic, most of it going east.

Some people were standing on the sidewalk, looking up and shading their eyes against the sun. There was a dogfight going on way up there between two fighter planes. It was the only dogfight I had seen during the entire war. The planes themselves could barely be made out, but the white condensation trails they left behind as they looped and twisted could easily be seen. We could also faintly make out, over traffic noises, the howling of engines and the faint rattle of machine guns.

I missed the actual moment when one of the planes was shot down because a large truck came by, towing a trailer with a V1 buzz bomb in it. This was a forerunner of the cruise missile and had received significant attention in the press as a "revenge weapon" against London. I was surprised by how cheap it looked.

When I looked up at the dogfight again, one of the planes had been shot down and now rapidly descended in a plume of black smoke. The interesting thing about this aerial combat was how few people even bothered to look up. No one cared any longer. Everyone went about their daily life, pretending that conditions were normal, and yet these were the people who had started the entire war.

I grew weary watching the coming and going of people in the Black Swan. Nothing interesting was happening. The traffic going by was also mundane, consisting mostly of soldiers in trucks. I set out walking along the street against the traffic.

Memmingen had an interesting town center. I had never seen an undamaged German town before. The houses were brightly painted in stripes or had heraldic designs on them. The inner town had changed hardly at all since the Middle Ages, as I later found out. The customary German flags flew outside the city hall, but the hysterical flurry of posters, urging everyone to fight to the last, was absent. A large brook meandered through the center of town. Three uniformed Hitler Youths leaned on the iron railing that bordered it. One examined a shiny black army pistol Model .08, and the other two held a hand grenade each. Their faces were earnest as they discussed something.

Further up the street, I came across a long line of people stretching into a side alley. I joined it and soon came to a warehouse where everyone was being given an oblong wooden box with a bright picture on it depicting a snowy mountain in the background and two Edelweiss flowers in the foreground. The box contained one kilogram of cheese.

Carrying my box, I continued up the street. It made a sharp turn and led out of the old city through a gate in the old city wall. There was a tavern called *zur Krone* (The Crown) facing the gate, with several small kids playing around the entryway to the tavern yard. I had been staring at them for several minutes when I realized one of them was my kid brother. For some reason, this did not surprise me at all. I asked him where our parents were, and he motioned inside the yard and resumed playing.

Once inside, I faced the old tavern stables. A reporting station lay to my right. *Meldestelle* proclaimed a sign outside, and, from time to time, two or three soldiers would enter and quickly leave again. Farther to the right, I found a building jammed with people. I walked into it and entered what was formerly a large beer hall. Heraldic designs and old targets hung on the walls.

A couple dozen mattresses were scattered on the floor and occupied by diverse individuals. Next to the windows lounged a boisterous group of four Frenchmen and one plump Frenchwoman. Further back were some Hungarians. My father lay asleep on a mattress next to one wall, and my mother sat on some bundles, staring straight ahead.

I walked up to her and handed her my box of cheese. She put it into one of the bundles and then stared at me all wet-eyed and started touching me about the shoulders, blubbering all the while about miracles.

"There was no miracle," I said. "They told me you had gone to Ulm, and I got on a train."

"But it's the middle of a war," she said, "in the middle of a foreign land. You're young; you just don't understand."

My father woke up and was appraised of his great good fortune in having me back. He did not look quite like the same man anymore. Something had gone out of him. He looked at me for a moment and touched my shoulder.

"So you are back," he said.

"I brought some cheese," I said by way of an excuse. Then I handed my field bottle to my mother, and easing my feeding bowl from under my shirt, gave her that, too. She put it with three others that the Germans had given them. Her bowls were slightly lighter gray and did not have a black stamp saying "Ideal" on the underside, as mine did.

"See, I told you not to worry," my father told my mother. "The Germans are an organized people. I knew they would get him back to us."

I went to sleep.

When I awoke, or rather was woken up, it was getting dark. There was one dim lightbulb way up under the ceiling. The light from it was so feeble that several groups of people had lit candles. Blackout curtains had been drawn.

The French group by the window were drunk and raucous. There were several murmured conversations going on. Most of the conversations had to do with the approaching allies and the end of the war. This again reinforced my immense contempt for the adults and their institutions. This same type of people had been loudly proclaiming the virtues of Socialism under Stalin, they had applauded Hitler's crusade against Communism, and now they were in the process of changing horses in midstream again.

My brother had come in from his playing and was hungry. My mother gave each of us a thin slice of stale bread and a small piece of the cheese I had brought. I reflected with some bitterness that I had managed much better all on my own.

Although there was a curfew, I slipped out the door in a panic, wanting to flee from my family. I had somehow never realized how helpless, pathetic, and unfit for survival they were. I did not wish to be saddled with them in the times to come.

Now that it was dark, the traffic to and from the *Wehrmacht Meldestelle* in the yard had increased. Soldiers were continuously checking in and walking out. I wished more than anything in the world to become one of them and to walk off into the night, leaving the clutter of my civilian life behind. I might even have persuaded myself to try it, but one of them chased me back into the room with the civilians.

The next day the main body of the Wehrmacht started to withdraw through Memmingen. It was a far cry from either their advance into the USSR or even their retreat on the Eastern Front. There were no tanks, no artillery. Trucks with tired-looking soldiers drove slowly down the narrow street. Some plump girls on the sidewalk flirted halfheartedly with a couple of officers in an open Kubelwagen. A few civilians and some disabled soldiers leaned against a building and watched the retreat.

Memmingen had been declared an "open city." I was not entirely clear on the concept, but although the city was full of retreating soldiers and there were American planes constantly overhead, not a shot was fired, not a bomb fell.

The retreat continued through the entire day. Towards the evening, I walked down to the brook at the center of town. A German Army truck was parked in a side alley, and a middle-aged soldier was handing large aluminum pots and serving ladles to three women who were rapidly carrying the stuff into a yard. They all stared at me. I knew that look well from both the USSR and the camp. It was the look of people who are doing something wrong and are afraid they will be reported to the authorities.

When I reached the brook, I was surprised to see several rifles and hand grenades lying on the bottom. The rifles had their stocks broken at the small of the stock where the shooter's hand grasps it while pulling the trigger. The sight of those broken rifles convinced me more than anything that the war was over.

American fighter aircraft continually circled a huge military airfield near Memmingen. I stood by the brook and watched the planes. One of them made a low pass at the airfield, followed by a cloud of exploding anti-aircraft shells from a 20 mm cannon. As I had observed several times before, the explosions were far behind the plane.

I walked back to The Crown. The army kitchen truck had disappeared from the alley. The retreat continued. A group of several soldiers and a sailor watched. I had never seen a sailor before, so he was an object of interest. None of these soldiers had any equipment.

Their attitudes were much more relaxed than those of the retreating troops. Soon curfew arrived, and I went back to the crowded hall and the drunk Frenchmen.

The retreat continued through the night. At times we heard some sort of heavy equipment going by. In the morning, the Meldestelle in the yard departed. A light truck drove up. Four soldiers loaded some boxes, a folding table, and some folding chairs into it and then drove away.

The innkeeper and his wife closed the heavy wooden gate across the entrance to the yard and disappeared. Two tiny American planes started circling the town. They were artillery-spotting planes, similar to the ones the Germans had for the same purpose, but smaller. Their engines sounded puny compared to those of the combat planes I been hearing for years.

We started hearing a few artillery shots. There would be a rapid series of four to six shots, a very long silence, and then another few shots. Everyone went into the hall and sat down. Since my return, I had acquired a great deal of independence from my family. I now exercised some of this by sneaking out and staring out at the road through a large crack in the gate. The road remained empty for a long time. Then a truck went by with a mortar and its crew in the back. Two trucks with infantry followed a few minutes later. Then there was another long wait.

Although the road was empty, I was far from bored, instead experiencing a sense of fear and anticipation. Several white sheets had been hung out of windows and dangled limply in the spring air. Finally, there came a sound of hobnailed boots, and a small group of soldiers passed. They walked far apart with large intervals between them. They walked as they had walked across all Europe, North Africa, and Asia Minor. Helmets tilted slightly, rifles slung across chests, hand grenades stuck into the tops of boots with the handles down and the heads sticking out the tops. Their faces were set with grim purpose. Then there was another short wait, and one last German walked by. He wore a cloth cap, had a machine pistol slung around his neck, and a hand grenade thrust diagonally behind the buckle of his equipment belt. That was all. All that had been familiar for all these years was gone. What would come next would be completely new and frightening.

At first, I almost missed them. There was just the cobbled street running slightly uphill and ending at the city gate, and the guard tower around and above the gate. The street ran between tall gabled houses. Slightly yellowed white flags hung out most of the windows. There was no wind and no sound except for the far away droning of the spotting planes circling high above the town.

Then there was a slight hint of movement, and suddenly, they were there. There were nine of them. Two were out in front walking on both sides of the street, one slightly in front of the other. They walked warily, their heads moving slightly as they peered at the doorways and windows and the white flags that hung from the windows. The first came to a turn in the street opposite my gate, where I peeked from between the boards. He stopped, holding out his left hand. The others froze. He then looked carefully around the corner, made a motion with his hand, and moved on. The others followed.

They walked in two extended files on either side of the street. Where the Germans had been greenish gray, with black belts and black boots, the Americans dressed all in green. Even the scabbards of their bayonets were green. They wore tall, round helmets. Their rifles appeared to have two barrels, one on top of the other. I held my breath, terrified I would be spotted behind my gate and killed. Then they passed me.

The silence returned. After what seemed like a long time, I heard the sound of engines. Two small vehicles came through the city gate. They looked like matchboxes on wheels. The first had a machine gun mounted on a post rising from the center of the vehicle. A box of ammunition had been fixed to the side of the machine gun. There were three people in this car. The second one had four people in it and trailed a long radio antenna.

As soon as the vehicles had passed, people appeared at the doors and windows of the houses. The tavern keeper and his wife opened the gate. Some civilians, including my father, came out of the old drinking hall and stood staring.

We heard the roar of motors, combined with a clanking, squealing noise. A tank rumbled through the city gate. It was tall, with a round turret that carried a short, stubby gun. Its front sloped steeply towards the turret. Its sides were flat and had a white star painted on them. A red flag hung from the turret. Another tank followed, and another.

Several large, open trucks carrying infantry came next. Machine guns were mounted over the cabs of the trucks and at the rear corners of the tailgates. Belts of bright copper ammunition hung out of the machine guns. The soldiers behind the guns looked grim. Two more tanks brought up the rear, each bearing a white star and flying a red flag.

The flags frightened me, reminding me of the Russians, but the white stars were reassuring since they were much like the ones I had seen on American planes.

Soon traffic flowed continuously through the gate. Tanks followed other tanks. I had never seen so many tanks in my life. Infantry rode atop many of the tanks. Except for the first group that had come roaring through at high speed, none of them had any red flags. There were also many halftracks. These were also shorter and stubbier than the German variety. Most of the halftracks were loaded with soldiers, but some carried quadruple machine guns with long, naked barrels.

This stream of armor squealed, roared, and rumbled past The Crown until evening and beyond. Around evening, vehicles began to stop, and soldiers appeared on the sidewalks. The German soldiers and sailor I had observed earlier now showed up again in civilian clothes. They seemed quite happy.

"You have lost the war," I said to them accusingly.

"Yes, and we are alive," replied one of them in a friendly fashion.

The street had now become crowded with German girls and women. They ignored German men but actively sought attention from the American soldiers. Other girls leaned out of windows and said things to soldiers passing on the sidewalk. Most of the conversations seemed centered around cigarettes.

It took me a few minutes to figure out that these women, whose men were still fighting and dying a few miles to the east, were offering to fuck their nation's enemies for a pack of cigarettes! At least our women in the USSR had the excuse of viewing the Germans as liberators and the fact that they were starving. But maybe that's all it was, an excuse. Maybe all women wanted to fuck men who conquered them. For the first time, I felt a slight inclination towards sympathy for the defeated German soldiers. It seemed to be a terrible injustice to have fought so hard and to have suffered hardships and committed atrocities and injured so many other people all for a pack of whores.

The women got bolder. One launched herself at an American and wrapped her legs around him while kissing him. They disappeared into a doorway.

Some military police soon arrived and large, white posters with the words "Off Limits" soon appeared on almost every door.

In the yard of our tavern lay an American. He was very young and very drunk. A puddle of urine surrounded him. The twelve-year-old daughter of a Lithuanian woman squatted above his face while her nine-year-old sister also squatted nearby. The twelve-year-old had her skirt pulled up with her crotch suspended just above the soldier's mouth.

"Would you stick your tongue in there, Johnny?" asked the girl. "Would you like to lick me there, you stupid drunk?"

Both girls giggled. The soldier tossed his head about and mumbled something in English.

"I bet you would like to stick your big prick inside me and tear me all up and make my pussy bleed, wouldn't you, Johnny? Only you can't because you're passed-out drunk. I could shit on your face, and you couldn't do anything. Does it feel good to be drunk and piss on yourself?"

The soldier tossed around and mumbled some more. He coughed, and vomit exploded from his mouth. The girl danced away.

"God, what a pig," she said to her sister.

A gaggle of refugee women, including my mother, were watching this scene.

"It's disgraceful," said some Russian lady. "You would never see a German soldier in that condition. Why doesn't someone stop this child? She is just like her mother."

Evidently the mother was off somewhere screwing Americans. The father sat in a corner among their bundles and looked surly; the entire group was pointedly and silently scorning him.

"Alex, that is a very bad girl, and I don't want you playing with her," said my father.

I could think of no fitting reply and tried to go to sleep.

The roaring and squealing of armored columns continued all through the night and into the next day.

The next morning, gangs of liberated eastern slave laborers flooded the town. They plundered and raped at will. The American military police could not cope with them.

I tried to attach myself to such a gang. After all, I had been one of them only weeks before. But that had been an age ago. I had thrown away my OST sticker and found my family again. I no longer belonged.

The group I attached myself to consisted of young people in their twenties. There were a few women present, though most of the gang was male. We walked down the middle of a cobbled street of the medieval German town like a herd of baboons, the stronger, dominant males in front and the weaker members, the women and me, in the rear. Passing Americans glanced at us incuriously; Germans got out of our way.

We walked with purpose. Our leaders had a goal. This turned out to be a small shoe store. The middle-aged German couple who owned it attempted to defend it. Some of the gang attacked and quickly disabled the couple. The man staggered away, clutching his bleeding face. The woman, possibly more fortunate, sat crying by the door as her face slowly began to swell.

We stormed into the store. The entire operation appeared to be highly organized. The taller members of our gang immediately jumped up on the counter that lined the walls of the store and began handing down boxes of shoes. In seconds, the shelves were bare.

I was completely shut out of the redistribution of wealth. All I could find was one shoe with a wooden sole. The shoes I already had were far superior to it, and it would not have fit in any case.

As we left the store, several American MPs arrived in their little boxy cars. They had small rifles with black magazines sticking out the bottom and slender, naked barrels. They fired a few shots into the air, and the gang scattered.

I walked down to the creek and watched a French motorized column crossing one of the bridges. Their uniforms and vehicles were identical to those of the Americans. The only difference was that some of the officers wore blue- or red-billed kepis. Some of these were quite ornate with leaves stitched around the hat in gold leaf. They looked out of place in this mass of tanks and halftracks.

On a nearby balcony stood two French sergeants. They were, like sergeants in other armies, sporting beer guts so that the belts in their trousers appeared to be in the process of cutting them in half. Underneath the balcony a dozen or so German civilians milled around. They stood like expectant dogs with their eyes fixed on the Frenchmen. At random times, one of the Frenchmen would toss a cigarette into the crowd. The crowd would seethe and boil. Tussles and fights would erupt. Then they would settle down again into still anticipation.

I did not like to see the humiliation of these Germans. It seemed petty and mean. Had a large number of them been rounded up and hanged as an example to the others, I would have accepted it readily. Governments and great leaders did things like that. But mean acts by individuals towards helpless people had always struck me as evil because they were done from weakness.

I wandered off through a break in the French column and followed the creek. It made a left turn through town and disappeared under a large, burned-out building. It emerged on the other side into a more rural setting. The town seemed to come to an end among widely scattered houses amid numerous trees and meadows. The day was very warm, and there were many flowers and butterflies.

In a small meadow next to a destroyed house, two Russian slave laborers were raping two German women. A Russian girl sat quietly nearby on a pile of bricks. Her skirt had fallen away from the lower part of her legs, exposing sexy thighs. She smiled at me in a sweet, angelic way. The two German women appeared to be mother and daughter. The daughter looked about fourteen. She was very skinny. There was blood all over her sparsely-haired crotch and all over the shaft of the huge prick that the Russian kept plunging into her. From time to time, her head would toss towards her mother.

"*Mutti es tut weh!*" said the girl.

The mother had had her head smashed in by a brick. It lay, bloody and glistening, at the feet of the second Russian who squatted nearby watching with what seemed like clinical interest. There was a large irregular depression on one side of the mother's head. One eye had filled with blood; the other eye rolled around like the eye of a frightened horse. Her heels periodically scrabbled at the ground, and her right arm twitched in an uncontrolled way. She made strange, rattling, hoarse sounds that were nonhuman and yet all too human.

The Russian who was watching her transferred his attention to me and made as if to get up.

"I am Russian, too," I said quickly.

"So what the fuck you want us to do, fuck you, too?" he said, but then settled back on his heels.

"*Mutti, es tut weh,*" said the girl.

"Goddamn it, I am losing it," complained the other Russian. "I can't concentrate with the old bitch making these noises."

The squatting Russian uttered a sigh, knelt next to the woman, took the bloody brick in both hands, and brought it down several times into the pulped side of the woman's head. The brick made a wet noise. The women's heels kicked very rapidly and then stopped. A sharp smell of shit arose.

"I can't do this, Kostia," said the other Russian, getting up and buttoning his fly. "Do you want her anymore?"

Kostia took two steps and bent over the daughter. His left hand went around her nose and mouth, turning her head. His right hand dipped into the pocket of his gray jacket and then emerged, making a cursory pass across the girl's throat. There was a quick explosion of blood, which he avoided. The whole act was elegant in its simplicity and casualness.

"Time to go," said Kostia. The Russian girl gave me another angelic smile and stood up. The three of them strolled away across the meadow. I followed. After a few steps, I turned around and looked back. A depression in the ground concealed the mother. The daughter looked like a bundle of drab clothes with artificial-looking skinny legs sticking out.

I turned again to follow the Russians.

"Get the fuck away from us, kid," warned Kostia. The Russian girl smiled at me again. I continued to follow. Kostia ducked down, picked something off the ground, turned around and threw. I sat down on the ground. My left shoulder felt numb. An egg-sized rock lay in front of me. My forehead broke out in a cold sweat, and my vision grew dim. I made out the figures of the Russians strolling away like people in a dream.

I sat in the meadow and tried to organize myself. My shoulder started to hurt. It was a new type of pain, a kind I had not felt before. It was deep and intense, growing sharp when I moved my arm. I discovered that it hurt less when I put my left hand between the buttons of my jacket and grasped the edge of the jacket. Looking like a young version of Napoleon, I made my way back to The Crown and lay down.

I stayed down for the rest of that day, alternately feeling sorry for my sore shoulder and trying to make some sense of the rape and killing of the two German women. The Russian girl, who had smiled at me, was far prettier than the women who had been killed. Why had the Russians bothered, when they could have fucked someone so much nicer and friendlier? It simply did not make sense. I finally shrugged it off as another peculiarity of the adults.

In the evening, my mother brought a Russian nurse who was staying at some other refugee shelter. The woman poked around my shoulder, causing a lot of pain, and declared that I had a broken collarbone.

"It's not a very important bone, and most boys break them," she explained to me. "Don't play or do anything silly, and it will grow together again and be much stronger." Then she talked to my mother in a more somber voice and departed. Since my injury was apparently not serious, I went to sleep.

Gunfire awakened me early in the morning. My first thought was that the Germans had returned and were retaking the town, but the shots were spaced far apart as if only one gun was firing. Also, the adults in the place seemed unperturbed. I got up and went into the courtyard.

Several American soldiers had a small caliber rifle and were shooting the pigeons that roosted under the roof. A few birds lay dead. Others fluttered about, surrounded by feathers and crimson droplets of blood. I picked up two birds with the one hand I could use and went back inside. Seeing that it was safe to go out, a couple of adults went out and picked up the other birds. I was furious that I could not use both hands. Two pigeons did not go far for the four of us.

Later in the day the French contingent, who still occupied the best part of the hall, began to bring in cars. They would wander away and return driving a civilian car. At one time there were six cars crowded into the small courtyard.

The Frenchmen explained to us that they were going to drive back to France in these cars. However, some MPs soon arrived and made them take the cars back to wherever they had been stolen. This apparent setback did not delay their plans for a return, as later in the day a large French amphibious truck pulled up in front of the tavern. The Frenchmen were whisked away to their and everyone else's relief.

There was a rush for the vacated space in the hall. Two families managed to secure choice spots. By chance, they turned out to be Russians, but a very different kind of Russian. These were Monarchists who had fled during the Revolution. They were cultured, conceited, and hostile. One family had two children about my age. After ascertaining my parents' professions, their parents allowed their kids to talk to me. The kids informed me that their father had been doing something "important" for the Germans, and that as soon as things got back to "normal," they were going to emigrate to Argentina where all the decent people were moving to escape from the Jews and Communists who now ruled the world.

I was quite puzzled by these kids. They were like no one I had ever met before. They were well-mannered, clean, and incredibly naïve. I found them uninteresting, and they found me common. My getting to know them made me feel that perhaps there had been some justice to the Revolution after all.

I tried to make friends with the girl who had been squatting above the drunken American's face. But when I suggested that we have sex, she said that she would only do it for cigarettes. She said that she had fucked an American for six cigarettes and that it had hurt. Besides, she explained, her mother only fucked for cigarettes.

My brother kept pestering me to play with him. He was only six years old, and our interests and lifestyles could not have been more diverse. To pacify him and my mother, who kept telling me to pay some attention to him, I took him for a walk around the town.

There was a strip of parkland running around the outside of the city wall. A paved walkway ran through the middle of it, and there were wooden benches at intervals. We walked slowly, observing the action. Girls and soldiers sat on the benches and lay on the grass. Used condoms littered the ground. Girls and soldiers strolled in pairs, smiled, and made deals. An incurious army patrol walked by, their carbines slung, cigarettes dangling from their lips.

An old German woman pushed a wheelchair in which her son sat. He had lost both legs and one arm up to the elbow. His scarred face bore a look of hatred and malice. He wore his old SS tunic to which were pinned an Iron Cross and a wound badge. He started abusing two girls who were walking with American soldiers, calling them whores and traitors. The girls yelled back that he certainly couldn't do a woman any good since his dick had probably been shot off as well.

The mother joined in berating the girls. The two Americans stood about for a while and then slowly tipped over the wheelchair, tumbling the wounded German onto the lawn. Then they and the girls walked off.

The mother ran around in circles, yelling and begging for help. Finally, some other girls left their Americans long enough to lift the German back into his wheelchair. After witnessing this, my brother asked to be taken home again.

When we returned to The Crown, there was a commotion going on. The mother of the two Monarchist kids was crying and screaming. The father yelled at the boy. The girl cried and cowered in a corner. The kids had collected used condoms for the girl to make raincoats for her dolls. The parents had caught them washing out the condoms by the tap in the courtyard. The kids had not known what condoms were. I started to laugh and got some furious looks from assorted adults. Later I tried to explain what condoms were and how they were used to the girl, but she stuck her fingers in her ears and refused to listen. I called her a stupid little bitch, and she ran to complain to her mother. I ducked out into the street.

Bemused by recent events, I followed the old highway, wishing intensely that I were still on my own. I slowly became aware of Russian being spoken. A group of six Soviet soldiers walked towards me. They were dressed partly in bits of Soviet uniforms and partly in American ones.

"Are you the Red Army?" I asked.

They surrounded me. "You are Russian. What are you doing here? Where are you from?"

I explained I was from Kharkov and had been in a work camp. They, in turn, told me their hometowns and gave me some American chocolate. It seemed there was a major *Stalag* (POW camp) near the town. Now that they had been liberated, they had come to town to "fuck some German women." They said the Americans were giving them more food than they could use and that I should come visit them at the camp and bring a large bag.

The next day, I emptied one of the bags we had carried our possessions in and started walking towards the camp. It was considerably farther than I had anticipated. I kept encountering groups of Soviet and Serbian ex-prisoners, walking in the opposite direction.

At first glance, the camp looked forbidding. There were two tall barbed-wire fences. The ground between the fences was covered with a carpet of interlaced barbed wire. A clear strip of ground ran along the inside of the fence. This had been the "death zone," and any prisoner setting foot within it was shot from one of the guard towers.

The towers themselves looked crude and sinister. They were shacks built up on poles with a roof, but open towards the camp. I climbed the ladder up to one of them, nursing my sore shoulder all the while, and found it empty.

Rows of unpainted barracks stood inside the barbed wire. Soviet, Serbian, Polish, and Italian flags flew above the barracks. The Soviets were the most numerous prisoners. The Italians were the fewest. I walked into the first Soviet barracks and someone yelled at me in broken German. I yelled back in obscene Russian. A soldier lifted me to the top of a tier of bunks and handed me a chocolate bar. I had to tell my life story. Then some of the prisoners went out and brought back people from other barracks who were from my home town. We talked for hours. At the end of it, someone lifted me off the bunk and set me down gingerly on the floor. My bag had been filled with US Army C-Ration cans, and a strap had been rigged so that I could carry it slung over my uninjured shoulder. They asked me to return the next day, and I left for town.

The walk was difficult. My sore shoulder hurt because of the injury, and my other shoulder started to ache because the strap of the heavy bag cut into it. I had to stop and rest frequently. At one point, an American jeep stopped. The soldiers in it tried to ask me something. We gave up because mutual language barriers made communication impossible. They drove away, and I continued my limping progress towards town.

When I finally got there, my mother was ecstatic over the rations. Afterwards, when I went outside to talk to the Lithuanian girl, my mother gave half of them away to two other Russian families. I was quite upset by this since I considered the stuff to be my property.

"You can't let people starve," explained Mother. "Professor Ivanov is an academician. He is a brilliant man."

"If he's so goddamned brilliant, let him get his own food," I said rather loudly. People stared. My father sat quietly on his bedroll and looked at the ground. I went outside to watch the whores picking up soldiers.

As I prepared to go back to the camp the next day, someone walked in and said the war had ended. I sat down for a moment but then walked to the creek. It was still full of broken rifles and grenades. I stared at them and tried to understand what peace meant. I felt as if I had been left stranded on a shore with the tide rapidly receding. I did not belong in this new world. I wanted to die, but I had to go back up to the camp and get more rations. I went back to the tavern, picked up my bag, and set out.

9

It is, I suppose, given to us to achieve a taste of success. Be it ever so transient, ever so ephemeral, we all must have at some time experienced the heady feeling that comes with the glimpse of our adequacy. Whether success comes at the cost of someone else, as in kicking the shit out of someone, or in the pursuit of some abstract goal, as in skipping a flat stone over seven times across a puddle, the rush of triumph is much the same. In our youth, this feeling is pure, unencumbered by guilt or compromise. I entered the success or entrepreneur stage of my life in June of 1945. It lasted for just about nine months.

My success was based on my association with the Soviet prisoners of war. The liberating American Army showered them with American rations. These were far more than the prisoners' needs. I became one of the beneficiaries of the surplus. Every day my brother and I would don German Army backpacks and walk the five miles or so to the camp. Here we would be received with incredible hospitality. We would make our way from barracks to barracks, our packs stuffed with C-Rations and ourselves filled with chocolate bars.

We would sit in on storytelling sessions, most of which were a bit on the macabre side:

"…so we were clearing off the dead bodies from in front of German machine gun positions. This was early in the war when we were attacking with bayonets, so there were hundreds of bodies. Anyway, they hadn't fed us for three or four days, and I found a can of salmon in tomato sauce on this one body. It had some blood spilled on it, and the body had been there for a few days, so it smelled pretty bad, but I washed it off in a puddle. Man, that salmon was the best-tasting thing I ever ate! I wonder if anyone who was drafted in the first year of the war is still alive?"

The consensus on that question was that probably no one was that lucky.

"Did they feed you pretty good at your camp, kid?" someone asked me.

"Got a piece of bread and some potato soup every day," I said.

"That's what we got," said the soldier. "You didn't have to work though, did you, being a kid?"

I informed him that, yes, I did have to work.

"And did they beat you if you didn't work fast enough?" was the next question.

I replied yes, they did.

"Fucking Germans," said the soldier. "We got to fuck their goddamn women and teach the motherfuckers what true socialism means."

"You fuck any of their women, kid?" asked someone else.

I said that I hadn't.

"We should take this kid into town with us and get him laid," said the first soldier. They discussed it but decided it was probably not a good idea since I did not have access to regular medical care, and should I get the clap, it would damage me physically and might warp my attitude towards women.

My brother, who was seven at the time, would sit quietly in a corner. From time to time, someone would hand him a piece of chocolate or a cookie, but he was regarded as being too young for serious conversation.

After a day of such social interaction, we would walk back to town, the backpacks agonizingly heavy, the sun unpleasantly warm, and sweat running into our eyes. Our parents would empty the packs and give some of the cans to their "friends." The numbers of these "friends" seemed to increase daily.

I was quite resentful of this situation. Most of the people that I was supporting conversed with my parents in a know-it-all adult fashion while ignoring me or disapproving of my unkempt appearance and casual social behavior. I was told several times that I did not behave as a boy of my social class should. I was graceless enough to tell them to fuck off, but I was also generous enough not to eviscerate them with a very sharp combat knife I had found and now habitually carried.

One day a refugee from Lithuania asked me why I kept giving the goods to my parents instead of selling or bartering them on the black market. The market was located a short distance from zur Krone, and it spread out over two or three city blocks. People with furtive expressions stood in doorways. These were the traders. Others, looking hungry and desperate, moved from doorway to doorway trying to barter bits of jewelry or watches for food, cigarettes, coffee, or evaporated milk. Coffee and cigarettes were the hottest items. Evaporated milk was also in great demand because women could no longer produce milk due to poor nutrition, and they needed the milk for their infants.

I quickly adjusted to this new and profitable reality. My parents were scandalized. Their number of "friends" ebbed in proportion to the free food my mother and father distributed.

Soon after I launched my career as a marketeer, there occurred one of those chance events that turn mere good luck into great opportunity. The Soviet prisoners at the camp received one hot meal at noon every day. This was prepared in a huge open-air kitchen under a canvas awning. A gang of German civilians scrubbed pots and fought over food remnants in the trash heap while sweating, red-faced Russian cooks attempted to turn American rations into borscht.

I happened to be talking to one of the cooks when an American Army truck arrived, and the Germans started to unload supplies. The cook ripped open the cardboard boxes, which for some reason were marked with a crescent moon, and classified the contents. One box contained rather pretty gold-colored cans. The cook stabbed a knife into one of the cans, and some brown powder came spilling out.

"Fucking coffee," he said. "Our people don't drink this shit. You want it, kid?"

I took the box, which was surprisingly light for its size, and took off before the cook could change his mind. I still wonder whether the man was stupid or whether this was an act of overwhelming generosity.

The Germans are a nation of avid coffee drinkers. Having been completely deprived of the stuff for the entire duration of the war, they were willing to trade anything for it. The two dozen cans I had been given were literally worth their weight in gold. Using them as capital, I could really begin to operate. And I did so with energy, verve, and enthusiasm. I swapped coffee for cigarettes, cigarettes for liquor, and liquor to GIs for more cigarettes.

Soon, the older, established dealers along the street knew my name. They pointed me out to people seeking items I was likely to have. Women approached me, requesting that I steer American GIs their way. Since the other dealers had German girlfriends, I followed their lead. It was gratifying to hand an adult woman a can of Spam or a pack of cigarettes and have her kneel in front of me and start slobbering and sucking on my dick. It was especially gratifying since these same women had considered me a subhuman animal only a few short months ago.

In terms of real income, I was probably one of the richest people in town. My parents were overwhelmed and frightened. Their remaining friends whispered accusingly and pretended derision they could not possibly have felt in their starving intellectual guts. Life was grand. And I was only twelve years old.

But war still hung in the air, only a synapse or microsecond away. When I tired of the black market, I would seek spiritual peace and a sense of balance in one of two places.

The first place was a huge military airfield that lay a few miles the other side of Memmingen. I would wander around among the bombed-out hangars and the destroyed aircraft and feel the icy grip of the war tightening around my insides. Bombs, aircraft cannon shells, and belts of machine gun ammunition and other equipment were scattered about in profusion. The hangars were always drafty, and the wind produced an eerie and melancholy sound, flapping bits of torn fabric under their roofs. Dead bodies still rotted away under piles of rubble. I wondered how once good-looking, vital young men could smell so horrible.

At times, I climbed into an ME 110 fighter plane, sat in the bare metal seat, and stared through the thick, exceptionally clear front windscreen. I moved the control stick and pretended to shoot down American bombers. I returned from these excursions feeling drained and peaceful.

The second place that brought me relief and solace was the railroad yard. The yard and the adjacent civilian homes had been bombed into a shambles so vast and utter that one did not at first grasp where the railroad ended and the homes began. There had been a lot of military traffic at the time of the raid, and military equipment of every description intermixed with the twisted rails, shattered rail coaches, and exploded homes.

Some of the bomb craters were the largest I had ever seen. They were full of water and the size of small fishponds. Life had quickly adapted to them. They were inhabited by populations of frogs. Large dragonflies flitted over the stagnant water.

An oppressive silence hung over the railyards. I suppose the place was still full of unexploded ordnance. There were certainly enough scattered German munitions to fight a battle. I climbed onto railroad cars that had four-barreled anti-aircraft cannons mounted on them. There I sat in the saddle behind the gun and twirled the cranks and wheels that made the gun move around.

The gun fired 20 mm shells. The explosive ones were painted yellow and had little aluminum nose caps that screwed off. The armor piercing ones were painted black and appeared to be solid steel. I picked up these shells by their long, shiny brass cases and banged the explosive heads on a steel rail until the shell had loosened in the cartridge case. I would then remove the shell and pull out the powder charge, which was in a small silk bag. The bag had a picture of Mickey Mouse coming out of a shell. I would burn the powder and think of the war.

A couple of troop trains had been in the station during the raid. Piles of bloody uniforms lined one section of rail. The blood had long since turned black, but the wadded up piles of darkened field-gray rags were a macabre reminder of a past that was quickly slipping away.

I could not determine the purpose of much of the military equipment. But it was all well-made, and I enjoyed unscrewing whatever bits of it would come apart.

Some of the houses around the edges of the bombed area were still standing. They looked as if they would fall down in the next strong wind. I entered and explored these places. In one house, I found a kitchen in which, miraculously, a full cupboard of china had survived. I started to carefully remove every thin plate, every delicate saucer, only to sail them out the window into the surrounding desolation below. There, tucked away in a gravy boat, I discovered a wad of brand-new, crisp Reichsmarks. This sudden revelation of the humanity of the former owner depressed me. It was the sort of thing my mother would have done. I put the money back, stopped breaking the dishes, and snuck out of the ruined home.

I hid my stash of black market goods among these ruins. I could not keep them around my parents since they were untrustworthy and out of touch with reality. They would have given away the food items to their friends and probably turned over the cigarettes to the authorities.

Among the houses that had been completely leveled, I discovered three serviceable basements. I gained entrance to these through tiny windows, so near the ground level they could have served as fire slits for bunkers. The basements of two of them were partly flooded. I concealed my goods beneath the rubble and then on exiting collapsed some more masonry over the access windows.

In one of the basements, a German soldier had changed into civilian clothes before desertion. His uniform and equipment lay in a corner. He had been a medic. His equipment belt bore a large leather satchel full of bandages and morphine. Attached to the belt was a heavy bayonet-dagger with a red cross inlaid in the handle. The blade had a saw-toothed back and a flat, blunted point.

For a time, my life had stopped being turbulent. I felt at peace and in perfect balance. If my black-market reality of starving Germans, greedy dealers, and sweat-stained whores began to wear on me, I went to the airfield or the railyards for relief. If the presence of war became too imminent and overpowering, I went to the market or the POW camp.

Then the camp began to be repatriated. Most of the prisoners looked forward to returning home, and most of them never made it. Early in the war, Stalin had issued an order that no one, military or civilian, was to allow the Germans to carry them off and use them as labor. We had all been ordered to commit suicide in the event that happened. All of us were now guilty of cooperating with the enemy. Some of those who returned were shot, others received fifteen years of penal servitude in Gulags.

One of the about-to-be-repatriated soldiers hugged me and said, "I know you don't understand this, kid, but try to remember us." I have never forgotten.

After the last of the Russians had left, the camp became a haunted place. I walked around the empty barracks and watched the wind whirling dust devils across the parade grounds. Soon, the Americans strung new barbed wire and filled the place with German prisoners. Once more machine guns pointed from the guard towers.

This was now a processing-out camp. The Germans were interrogated, then released. As they trudged down the highway, American guards stopped them and searched them. The Americans usually lounged by the side of the road in the company of a few German girls. The girls smiled and talked to the American soldiers, pointedly ignoring their bedraggled countrymen who were forced to open their backpacks and spread their meager belongings in the dirt for "inspection." From time to time, one of the Americans would disappear into the bushes with one of the German girls.

My family was moved from the tavern hall in which we had lived all this time to a private home overlooking the creek. A large blonde woman from Leipzig owned this home. Her husband had been in the Afrika Corps and was in some British POW camp. I gave the lady a small can of powdered coffee, and my mother wondered why our reception was not hostile. The woman had a boyfriend who had been a member of the Nazi Party and who now had a wonderful job clearing garbage from an American Army camp.

A movie house opened in town and started showing American films. I saw a rather stupid film with Veronica Lake and got an erection watching her stuff a grenade between her tits to blow herself up along with some Japanese soldiers. Civilization was slowly returning.

The war still kept its grip on the airfield and the railyard. Here I would play out my last bonding act with the war, one that would make me a part of the war rather than a mere survivor and victim.

One afternoon I was playing in the zone of ruins between where the railyards ended and the houses began. I had picked up two hand grenades of the type called *Stielhandgranate* by the Germans and "potato masher" by the Americans. While employed in farm labor in Austria, I had watched a detachment of the local Volkssturm practice with grenades of that type. There was a tin cap on the bottom of the handle, which could be unscrewed. A ceramic ball attached to a thick silk or nylon cord would then fall out of the handle.

Holding the grenade in the right hand and the ceramic ball between the mid-fingers of the left, a person could separate the grenade from the cord with a sharp, steady pull. This action ignited a powder-train inside the grenade. The person holding it then counted to three and threw. The grenade would blow up about seven seconds after the cord had been pulled.

The grenades that the Volkssturm had practiced with were painted red and had large holes drilled through the metal heads. Large, nickel-plated detonators would be screwed inside the removable head. After the grenade had been thrown, the thrower had to retrieve it, unscrew the head, remove the exploded detonator, replace it with a new one, and hand the grenade to the next thrower.

The two grenades I had picked up were the real thing. Their solid, heavy heads had been painted a grayish green. The long, smooth handles were made of unpainted wood. As yet unaware of the concept of latent homosexual symbolism, I stroked the handles, all the while wondering whether I would have the nerve to actually throw one of the things.

I put on a discarded helmet and, crouching just below the rim of a giant bomb crater, peeked over the edge. Only gratifying desolation stretched all around. Completely leveled and pulverized houses graded imperceptibly into the less pulverized houses, which in turn were backed by more conventional ruins of standing walls, chimneys, and half houses whose outer walls had been sheared away, exposing rooms. I pretended I was defending this landscape against the encroachment of peace. I had to bring back the war with all its sacrifice and slaughter. And to bring back the war, I had to throw the grenade.

I sprang from the bomb crater and scampered in a crouch toward the ruins. To avoid being shot by an imaginary machine gunner, I took cover in another crater. The helmet was far too tight and pain pulsed through my temples. I discarded the helmet. After the next sprint, which brought me to the undamaged foundation of an otherwise collapsed house, I abandoned one of the grenades.

Clutching the remaining grenade, I peeked around the corner of the foundation. In front of me, a partly collapsed building's basement floor remained mostly intact. There was even an unbroken window facing me. The entire building was outlined by the sun setting behind it. Its edges of broken masonry were fuzzy and golden. I unscrewed the cap from the bottom of the grenade handle. The ceramic ball fell out into the palm of my left hand. With a smooth movement, as if I had done it hundreds of times, I withdrew the cord, activating the grenade.

Suddenly, I noticed movement behind the window and, squinting against the sun, perceived an old woman scowling at me. A strange series of events now occurred. These events appeared to be outside of known time, and so they are not subject to the usual mechanism of forgetfulness. They are happening still on a golden, sunlit evening. I have no control over them at all. I am a bystander, a witness. I have no will and no control over my body.

My arm arches back and then snaps forward releasing the grenade. The grenade makes one full turn in the clear evening air. I can see the white handle and the gray-green explosive head. The grenade is partly into its second turn when it shatters the glass of the window and goes in. I fall and cover my head. There is a period, a very tiny interval of silence. I am beginning to hope that I am only playing and that nothing will happen. Then, the detonation. Small pebbles hit the outside of my hands, which cover my head. Then there is silence again. Normal time returns.

I ran. For some reason, running was no longer the effortless movement through the air that it had been for so many years. There seemed to be a syrupy heaviness to the atmosphere, an invisible stickiness that impeded my progress. I ran out of breath, gasped, and sweated profusely. Still, I made fair progress, streaking along clear stretches, worming and twisting my way through the rubble where bombed buildings had collapsed into the streets.

Near the inhabited part of town, I paused for breath. I leaned against the wall of a ruin and sucked air in sobbing gasps as painful as vomiting in reverse. Spots and fragments of images drifted and swirled. Then normalcy returned. I heard a child crying in the distance. The sound of a truck carried clearly from a nearby thoroughfare. I straightened up and tucked my wet shirt into my short pants. Then I walked out of the ruins into the civilized world.

The images of the old woman, and of the grenade turning through its trajectory towards the window, fell into place. They were merely the last fragments that completed the mosaic, which was my early life, and which was now behind me. I had completed my larval stage, I had spent some confusing time in a cocoon, and now I had emerged. I was no longer a victim. I had killed. I now belonged with the Red Army, with the disciplined gray ranks of the SS, with the silent green Americans I had watched invading the town. I had now made the war a part of me. It was my war, and it would never go away.

As I realized this, I stopped trudging and began to march. My shoulders went back, and my head came up. I gazed disdainfully at the shabby, starving civilians and smiled at the occasional American. One of them smiled back and threw me a cigarette. I flipped him a two-finger salute and gave the cigarette to a German civilian who was eyeing it enviously. I felt grown up, competent, and proud.

IO

I became far more efficient and hard in my black-market dealings. People who used to like me no longer did. To keep from being
taken advantage of by the mostly adult dealers and buyers, I got a
gun. I obtained it from an older kid who had found it, and I gave
him a large, sealed tin of chocolate for it. The pistol was a dull black,
very small automatic, caliber 6.35 mm. It had the word "MARS" on
its hard rubber grips. There were four shells in the magazine. The
cartridges were of light color, and a ring of delicate pink lacquer
surrounded the case mouths, sealing out moisture.

Oddly, as my pragmatism and cynicism increased, so did my
fantasy life. I looked forward to sleep because lurid dreams usually
accompanied sleep. I would wake up in the night covered with
sweat and either uncomfortably hot or shivering.

I gave up what friends I had for imaginary ones that felt far
more real. I read since then that it is quite common for children to
have imaginary playmates. I had battalions of them. In tattered uniforms, with shattered limbs, their entrails wound about their legs,
they hopped, tottered, and marched with me through my daily life.
I only had to glance away from some mundane occupation for an
instant, and I would be with them manning a machine gun in front
of Vienna, defending a burning Kharkov, or falling from the sky in
a disintegrating bomber.

All these playmates wore different uniforms. I could almost rec-
ognize some of them; the Russian who had shown me how to use
a Soviet grenade, the German with a machine pistol who had yelled
at me while I watched the Russian tankers burn and melt. Oddly
enough, none of my dead girlfriends or other civilians ever made
an appearance. I knew that it would only be a short time before I
would join all my imaginary friends, and that knowledge began to
insert itself between me and my daily life.

One day I was haggling with a German over a heavy silver signet ring that he was trying to exchange for cigarettes. I had several packs of Lucky Strikes and Chesterfields on my person and was in the process of completing a very satisfactory deal. A sudden warning shout arose. People began to disappear into doorways and to drop incriminating goods.

Two American jeeps with machine guns mounted on them had driven up and parked across one end of the street. An American Army truck blocked the other end. American MPs and German civilian police started frisking us and separating us into groups. They found my cigarettes, and, of course, they found my pistol. The MP who found the pistol asked me if I was German. When I told him I was Russian, he dropped the weapon in his pocket and told me to get in the truck. The other people in the truck tried to edge away from me, but there were so many of us that we were packed in tightly.

After a very short ride, we were herded into a holding tank in the back of a picturesque, medieval city hall. People kept coming to the door, calling out names, and the people whose names were called were led away. No one called my name, and I was left as the sole occupant of the large room. Finally, a German policeman came in and ordered me to go with him. We left the building, and he mounted a bicycle. I walked and trotted alongside. We went to the city hospital, where I was signed for by a grim-looking woman. I got a blood test, was x-rayed, had my chest thumped, and had to rub the head of my penis across several glass microscope slides. All of this was quite new to me and interesting.

After a while, my father arrived and took me home. He remained quiet and uncharacteristically non-abusive. My mother was also quiet and told me I would be leaving the next day for a stay in a sanitarium. I had no idea what a sanitarium was, and my parents tried to explain it to me. It sounded rather fun, like a sort of summer camp.

The place was called Bad Wörishofen. It had been a spa for wealthy Europeans. Now it was a staging place for young Jews going to Palestine. Ranks of them marched and countermarched across a parade ground. Two doctors, Caplan and Phillipovitch ran the place. Caplan was balding and stout; Phillipovitch was tall and skinny. It soon became obvious that the Jewish kids were not the only shipments destined for Palestine. Piles of German Army equipment kept appearing and disappearing.

The food in the place was great. No one much bothered about the few other Russian kids and me. Shortly after arriving, I was given a shot of some sort. For the rest of the time, I would roam the grounds in the company of a slightly older kid, or we would climb over a wall and explore the surrounding woods.

After about six weeks, my father showed up and took me away. Once more, I went to the city hospital in Memmingen to be bled, x-rayed, thumped, and urine tested. The nurse who took me through all these operations was a young nun with a truly angelic face. I got an erection thinking of her and couldn't piss for the urine test.

This time, they wouldn't let me go home and kept me at the hospital overnight. It seemed that I had TB. The next morning, another German policeman took me to the now somewhat fixed-up rail station and put me on a train for Kempten.

Kempten is a small town in the Alps. The TB sanitarium was quite different from Bad Wörishofen. For one thing, the food wasn't as good, and for another, the patients were much quieter. The scenery, however, was magnificent. I would stare for hours at the granite masses of the mountains and watch the play of light and shadow across them.

In the camps, TB spelled certain death. I had no idea the disease could be stopped, and I awaited death with quiet contentment. I still had my company of imaginary friends and looked forward to becoming one of them. They were far more real to me than the daily routine of the hospital. I tried explaining all this to my mother during one of her visits, and the silly woman burst into tears and ran off to talk to the doctors. As a result, the staff watched me more closely than the other kids, and I could not have a knife during meals.

One of the other kids was a Polish blonde. She was stocky and well equipped with tits and freckles. She also had seductive green eyes. The basement of the hospital contained a room filled with French Army gas-mask bags. We would meet there and, climbing on top of the bags, make out. I kept trying to screw her, and she kept asking me if I would marry her if she got pregnant. On one occasion, I had my hand in her pants and my tongue in her ear. I had one hell of a hard-on and could smell her pussy. Success seemed imminent. Just then, we were surprised by an old nurse. She marched us to a lab, and there we were subjected to several VD tests. The girl never spoke to me again.

After nine months at the sanitarium, my TB was contained. It did not go away. I was not cured. It simply stopped eating my lungs. I stopped coughing and trying to bring up blood, which would have enabled me to join my ghostly companions. It was over.

The doctors discharged me from the sanitarium. I left and caught the train back to Memmingen. It seemed that I would have to live in a peculiar new world after all. The prospect did not make me happy. I hated having to change my plans.

I arrived home rather morose. My father had just gotten a job teaching plant pathology and was his old arrogant self. My family drew liberal food rations from the International Refugee Organization. The black market had changed, and my old caches near the railroad yards had surely been discovered since the entire area was being rebuilt.

One day, my father pulled me aside.

"I am deeply ashamed of you," he said. "For months you did shameful things that no boy of your social class should even know about, let alone engage in. To my unending sorrow, I did not stop you."

"You never stopped eating, either, you son of a bitch," I shouted. He belted me across the mouth, and I grabbed a kitchen knife.

"Would you cut your father?" he asked.

"I'm going to cut your balls off," I promised, charging at him. We did several laps around the kitchen table with my mother shrieking and wailing at us in accompaniment. We stopped when we ran out of breath.

"You will be going to a German school next week," my father promised grimly. "They will knock some sense into you. You are a subhuman, just as they said. They knew what they were talking about."

And so, I went back to grammar school. On my first day, the school director explained that, although I had only been to the first grade, my age and my father's "station in life" enabled me to enter the fourth grade. The director hoped I could cope with the work.

The teacher was an old nun. After assigning me to a seat, she had me extend my hands, palms downward. Then she hit me sharply across the knuckles with a ruler. "You have filthy fingernails, you little Russian pig," she said. The German kids tittered.

The long vacation was over.

—Sally Panasenko

Up until now, Alex Panasenko has been a slave laborer in Nazi Germany, a factory worker, a soldier in the US Army during the Korean War, a graduate student in Entomology at UC Berkeley, a science instructor at Berkeley High School, and a bartender. In only a few more years, he will be one hundred, at which point he plans to decide what to do with his life. In the meantime, he is biding his time cooking for wife Sally and dog Lucy in Portland, Oregon.

CPSIA information can be obtained
at www.ICGtesting.com
Printed in the USA
FSHW010506221221
87114FS